Far County Chronicles
A Texan's Perspective

by

Jack Everton

DORRANCE PUBLISHING CO., INC.
PITTSBURGH, PENNSYLVANIA 15222

Dorrance Publishing Co., Inc.
701 Smithfield Street
Pittsburgh, PA 15222
Visit our website at *www.dorrancebookstore.com*

ISBN: 978-1-4349-2534-3
eISBN: 978-1-4349-2137-6

Dedication

For Bob and Jim.

Preface

My Aunt Kitty wrote me some time ago to ask if all the stories in this modest collection are true. "Of course, they are!" I wrote her back. And they are, at least from my point of view. I read somewhere that truth is, for the most part, a matter of location, and my present location is about ten thousand miles away from most people who might take umbrage with some of my tales. Ten thousand miles is a good head start and may be necessary to use in order for me to run from the real truth, but I sincerely hope not.

I have taken some liberties with names, offices, and deeds, especially in Beirut, but many of those who might be most offended are probably not with us anymore. All of these stories have been written from my own memory, some of them from almost sixty years ago, and I'm sure there are mistakes and omissions and lapses of one kind and another, and I apologize for those. But these incidents and my recollections of attitudes and feelings are as true as I can make them, and I hope you find as much pleasure in reading them as I have found in writing them.

Jack Everton

Steel-Drivin' Man

Like John Henry, my daddy was a steel-drivin' man. He stood an inch under six feet and weighed between two hundred forty and two hundred fifty pounds, depending on how much of Mom's chicken-fried steak, homemade biscuits, cream gravy, and beer he'd consumed the day before. He had arms as thick and tough as the oak logs we burned in the fireplace, and although he was a lawyer, he could swing a single-bit ax and a 16-pound sledgehammer about as well as anybody I ever came across. Lawyers were different in those days.

He was born in Indian Territory in the sandy dirt just a few miles north of the Red River and with his older sister and parents, migrated throughout Oklahoma and Texas following oil boom and bust. His daddy was a driller, a piano tuner, and if I remember correctly, he played the violin quite well. Drillers were different in those days.

After seventeen years of nomadic wandering and working, Dad's high school graduation found him in Yoakum. It's a tiny town located about a hundred miles due east of San Antonio, where in springtime, the air reeks of bluebonnets and oil—not a bad combination once you get used to it. Then for three years, he worked as an able-bodied seaman on tankers traveling from the Gulf Coast to New York City and spent some time as a roughneck down in Refugio. One fall, he decided to enroll in that august institution of higher learning in Austin and left it a few years later with a degree in law.

After graduation in 1937, he moved to the West Texas town of Knox City, where he opened a law office. Why he chose Knox City, I don't know, but I'm glad he did. He started courting a country school teacher there who was later to become very important in my life. For one thing, she gave it to me.

The West Texas law business was not flourishing in those days and just before he starved to death, Dad was made an attractive offer by several businessmen from McGregor in McClennan County. They needed a lawyer in their fair city. He accepted their offer and moved two hundred fifty miles to the southeast.

His financial situation improved in the new location, but after a short time, he realized that all of Central Texas in general, and he in particular, would benefit from the presence of the pretty little school teacher he had left behind. He called and she said yes, although she was a little concerned about how he would transport her and her belongings all that distance. "Don't worry," he said. "I've caught a ride with a load of mules. I'll be the one with the red rose." I'm sure that was comforting to Mom.

For once, though, he didn't go with the mules. After turning down the loan of a new Chevrolet, he got in his old Model A, drove to Knox City, picked up his bride, and brought her to the house. Later, Mom confided in me that "his car was nothing but an old rattletrap!"

Dad's practice prospered and they saved their money. After three or four years, they bought one hundred twenty acres a few miles south of Temple. He moved his wife and sons to Bell County, and that's where I grew up—if you can call it that.

I loved the country homestead and spent every possible minute outside. A short wooden cot stick served as my Winchester 30-30, and I carried it with me at all times. I'm sure the entire acreage is still strewn with the bodies and bones of the tens of thousands of cowboys, Indians, pirates, and knights I indiscriminately slaughtered. Of course, I retired undefeated. Heck, I never even got captured.

Perhaps my fondest childhood memories generally surround the late afternoon, when all my adversaries had retired from the field and I sat on the front porch with my wooden rifle, waiting for Dad to come home. I'd see him top the last hill about a mile away and rush up the dirt road to meet him. When I got close enough, he would stop the car to let me climb on the right-front fender for the last few hundred yards. This was a practice we continued for a couple of years, and I'm sure it drove him nuts.

In the winter months, after he got home, he would go inside the house, change clothes, and head for the garage to get the axes, sledges, and wedges. Then we would march to the wood pile and begin cutting and splitting the oak and pecan limbs we had gathered throughout the year into fireplace-sized logs. He would swing the heavy ax with practiced authority, and when it came in contact with the hardwood, it would ring and sing with such power and beauty that John Henry himself would have been proud. I picked up the chips. Sometimes after we were finished, he would gather me in his arms and hug me as he carried me to the house for our supper. The smell of his shirt, the wood, cigar smoke, sweat, and the feel of his rough cheek against my own was wonderful.

It's been over half a century now, but the ax and hammer still ring for me. Pretty soon we're going to meet again. I'll bring my ax, which I guarantee you will shave the hair off anything that stands still. I'll show him I can trim a fence post almost as well as the finest cedar chopper in Palo Pinto County. He'll like that.

Scissor-tailed Flycatchers and the Jerk

Our house in the country had a white wooden fence around it. The fence was made of cedar posts and one-by-sixes, and it was quite distinctive and handsome. When giving directions to folks who wanted to visit us, we'd always say, "It's the big white house with the white fence around it." It was very easy to see when driving out South 31st Street Road. Oh (I almost forgot), "And you can't miss it."

It came as a very rude shock to me, when we painted the fence one time, that the fence had two sides—the inside, which we got to look at and enjoy, and the outside, for people passing by. It didn't seem fair that we had to scrape and paint both sides. It was a hell of a job, especially in the summer, and it was twice the job that I thought it was going to be when I agreed to do it. Actually, it was a family project that we all pitched in to do with my mom as the big boss and enforcer.

Within the fenced yard, we had room enough to play football and baseball, park the five or six cars we used when we all got big enough to drive, and do just about anything we wanted, except shoot. Rabbits and quail were the main beneficiaries of this no-shooting-in-the-yard rule, and it took me a while to appreciate the safe zone that my father insisted on. Sometimes a whole covey of Bobwhite Quail would pass through the yard, and I would run to my dad and tell him that I could kill at least four or five with one shot if he'd just let me have the chance. "Inside the fence, all game should feel safe. It's not fair to shoot them around the house. If you want to shoot quail, you'll have to go out in the fields and track them down in their own territory. Not here." Now, that didn't seem fair to me, because when I'd stumble upon quail out in the fields, they'd burst from cover with their machinegun drumming of wings that never failed to give me a heart attack. By the time I'd recover from my fright and get the .410 to my shoulder, they'd be one hundred twenty yards down the field—too far for a shotgun.

But one time, I was outside in the yard with my BB gun, and I saw a pair of Scissor-tailed Flycatchers sitting on the electrical line that went from the house down to the pump shed at the well. The scissortails were outside the yard, about thirty feet from the fence. I slowly crept up to the fence and propped the gun on one of the white rails to steady my hold on the rifle, took careful aim, and pulled the trigger. The BB caught the closest bird squarely in the breast, and it fluttered down to die on the ground directly below the electric line. The other bird was obviously shocked and dismayed, and it followed its mate to the ground to render aid and assistance, but to no avail.

It flew away as I approached to examine my kill, but did not, and would not, go far from the body of its cherished companion. It took me almost twenty years to realize the enormity of my ruthless, senseless deed.

Guns and Rags

Growing up in the country in Central Texas, I was surrounded by guns. My daddy was about the finest wing shot I ever saw, and I suppose all boys say that about their dads, but I really mean it and I'm telling the truth. He had an old Browning 12-gauge automatic with a full choke, and every fall we'd spend many a late afternoon sitting on a stock tank waiting for the mourning doves to come in for water. They'd dive down at fifty-five miles an hour, dodging and feinting, and you had to be able to shoot to hit one. Dad never missed—not that I remember, anyway—until I was almost eighteen and had moved to the ranch in Bosque County. In those days, Dad was getting older and didn't see so well anymore, and the hand-eye coordination was beginning to slow down. He would drive up to visit me, and we continued to hunt doves, but he would hit only three out of four. "I used to shoot pretty well," I remember his saying. With doves on the wing, I never got past one in three. He never said, but I could tell that he was somewhat disappointed in my poor shooting.

As a child, I started out with a Red Rider BB gun (It went well with my first-grade Red Rider lunch box, both signed by Red Rider himself), and every day I walked throughout the trees and pastures, shooting at anything that moved. After a year or two of that, all the wild animals on our property became very cautious and wary of my perpetual presence, and it took considerable skill to get close enough to any creature to shoot it with an air rifle.

When I was eight or nine years old, I graduated to an old Winchester pump .22 rifle and a side-by-side .410 shotgun (both with exposed hammers), which allowed me to kill at long range, and my hunting routine changed drastically in that I didn't have to sneak around and crawl behind bushes and such to get close to my intended prey. With my new weapons, if I could see'em, I could shoot'em. Dad taught me how to treat the guns with the utmost respect, how to cross a fence when armed, how not to shoot a rifle in the air, how not ever to point a gun at anybody, and when the time came, how not to shoot your hunting partner. All these rules I followed perfectly and would do so this day if I had occasion to pick up a gun again. He was a good teacher.

I loved the guns and my constant canine companion, Rags. He was a great natural retriever and for three or four years, we were inseparable. The guns and dog were welcome equalizers for a small person, and because we lived with no close neighbors, at night there were no lights to be seen anywhere, and sometimes it got scary out there. From time to time, I found myself home alone at night and I would get the rifle, load it, and sit on the sofa in front of the fireplace with the gun across my lap and Rags at my side. I knew that Rags would warn me if anything were amiss, and the rifle made me about as tough as anybody in the county. With Rags and the rifle, I was not afraid. When I would see the lights and hear the engine of one of our cars coming home, I would quickly unload the gun and put it back in the corner of the bathroom closet. I don't think anyone ever knew I did that, except Rags, and I knew he wouldn't tell.

When I turned fourteen, I bought my first pistol, an Iver Johnson, nine-shot .22 caliber revolver. Dad was not happy about my purchasing a hand gun. "Too dangerous," he said, but I could legally buy the gun and I had my own money, and he kept his mouth shut about it all and, as in most things, continued to be a good example, rather than boss too much. Besides, I had been hunting almost daily for seven or eight years, and I was an experienced outdoorsman and had learned my gun safety lessons well. I kept that pistol for over thirty years, and it served me well. It had the sweetest, softest trigger and was extremely accurate up to a hundred yards. I once shot a fox with it, a running shot at 120 yards, at night—and it wasn't all luck. There are other stories to tell about that gun and its usefulness, but I'll save them for another day.

Until I moved to Bosque County, a great deer-hunting area, I had never fired a high-powered rifle, and to prepare me for my new hunting education, Dad bought me an old sporterized 7.65 mm Argentine Mauser, vintage 1891. I would have preferred a Marlin or Winchester lever action 30-30, but one doesn't look a gift horse in the mouth and I accepted The Mauser with pleasure. I found out later that the lever actions looked good in the movies and were very practical at short range in brushy country, but they didn't shoot like the bolt action gun. The Mauser had a vicious kick, and if I could keep from flinching when I pulled the trigger, it was deadly accurate at five hundred yards. It shot hard and straight and packed a wallop from the muzzle end as well. I never really tested it at a distance of over 500 yards, because anything that was coming after me and was still that far away I could probably outrun. Five hundred yards is a substantial head start.

All my bragging about proper gun etiquette and ability notwithstanding, there were two instances when I made major mistakes: The first was shooting a hole through the bathroom wall when I was about eight years old (I got a spanking for that one), and the second was at the ranch when I shot an "unloaded" 30-30 through the main bedroom wall downstairs. This second occasion would not have been so bad except that the powerful bullet entered the living room closet as it left the bedroom and put a bullet hole, front and back, through all the coats, shirts, and jackets Dad had hanging on the rack, and then proceeded through the other closet wall to fly across the living room, where it landed, spent, on the west-side windowsill. Dad laughed it off and I was too big to spank. Throughout my career, I shot a hole in my bedroom ceiling at the old home place and plugged a mattress and a chest of drawers while I was at it—not all at the same time, of course. "I must have taught you well," my dad once commented. "At least you never shot anybody." I must confess that I've thought about shooting a few people, and I've met a couple of guys who needed shooting, but he was right. I never did shoot anybody. Not yet.

After my high school graduation, I entered Baylor University that fall and my hunting activities declined. I still took care of the livestock on the weekends, but I had little time for the hunting pursuits, which had been such an important part of my life. Sometime after my senior year in college, I quit killing things. It was not a conscientious or moral decision, at least I don't remember it as such, but I finally figured out that all feathered and furry creatures had a right to live and breathe as long as they could, just like me. Who was I to cut their lives short, just for the hell of it? Since that time, I have bought a few shotguns and a rifle, and I've gone hunting with every one of them, but I have never pulled the trigger. Somehow I have outgrown it all.

Milking

Four years before the rains would come again to Central Texas, it was my job to gather our Jersey cows, Hazel and Cissy, in the pasture and bring them to the barn for milking. My two older brothers did the actual milking, and every day in the late afternoon my dog, Rags, and I would go out and circle 'round behind them and drive them gently to the barn. It was not a difficult job most of the time, but I always took my air rifle along with us, just in case.

Early one evening, after I had put the cows in the lot and returned to the house, I mentioned to Dad that my brothers were not in evidence and that the cows were lowing and that they needed to be milked as soon as possible.

"There's the bucket over on the kitchen counter," he replied. "You'd better go down and get started."

He left the room before I could protest that I had never milked a cow in my life, and I was only eight years old, and that it was dark down there—and dangerous! No matter, my protests would have made no difference, anyway.

I went into the kitchen and put some warm water in the bucket to wash the cows' teats, left the house, and began my long, one hundred-yard walk to the barn. It was now quite dark and there was no welcoming light down at the barn. I had to turn on the light when I got there. The path to the barn passed by the chicken house, and I had it on excellent authority that there were wolves and bears behind there and that they would eat me on the spot if I came too close. My spirits were greatly encouraged by Rags and the three or four cats who followed along behind in single file. The cats were not in the least concerned with the wolves and bears behind the chicken house or the man-eating tiger that was waiting for me in the feed room. I knew Rags would warn me if anything was suspicious or dangerous. I didn't count on the cats. Cats are not dependable if wolves attack. They will take care of themselves only and the devil (or wolves) take the hindmost.

We passed the chicken house without incident and entered the barn by the main gate. I put each cow in a separate stall, climbed high up on the heavy wooden fence between them, and reached out and pulled the light cords on the two naked bulbs, which hung over each stall. Now came the tricky part.

During the actual milking, we always gave the cows some special food to keep them happy, still, and contented while we robbed them of most of their calves' supper. Unfortunately, the special feed was located inside the feed room behind a door that opened to the darkest and most dangerous place in the entire county. Opening that door was always risky. You never knew what would jump out at you as soon as the slightest glimmer of light, and breath of fresh air and freedom appeared between the jamb and the door's edge. Inside, hay was stacked as high as the roof; saddles and ropes and other paraphernalia were on the right, and the food bags were on the left as you went in. The single light in the large room was located high above the door, and to turn it on, you had to climb up the open, horizontal braces between the wall studs to screw in the bulb. The light was about twelve or thirteen feet above the floor, and as you climbed up the wall, your back was exposed and completely unprotected, and your vision was limited to the dusty wall in front of you, a distance of some four or five inches, and about a yard or two on the right and left.

In all my life, I have never felt as vulnerable as I did when climbing up the side of that feed room wall. And it was not without reason. All haylofts are rife with rats and mice, snakes, raccoons, spiders, and I-don't-know-what-all and, on occasion, man-eating tigers. As I climbed the wall, my ears could pick out the rustlings of a hundred varmints repositioning themselves due to the unexpected intruder and his dog. Rags would always enter the feed room first to take on all comers who would attempt to do us harm. He was fearless and undefeated (except for once).

On that night, I poured a generous helping in the mangers for both cows, placed my stool next to Hazel's right-rear leg, and sat down. I chose to begin with Hazel, because she was older and more patient than Cissy and had some sense. Cissy was only a couple of calves past being a heifer and was still a little bit goofy.

I washed Hazel's teats and dried them with the clean towel I had brought from the house. I then grabbed one in each hand and squeezed. Nothing. I tried again a few more times with the same result. Perhaps I had started with the wrong ones. Hell, I didn't know. I shifted slightly on my stool and changed over to the other two in a move that was a cross between a defensive chess maneuver and the South Texas border roll. Still nothing, or almost. A few tiny drops came out and splattered down on the bottom of the empty bucket. I shouted with enthusiasm and the expectant cats, who were seated in a row, side by side, about three feet away, were grinning. I felt Hazel's leg move a bit, and she looked back at me with a disgusted sneer that I will never forget. "Who have they sent down this time? A boy to do a man's job." She turned back and continued eating, but I could tell that she was working hard to be patient.

After about thirty minutes of squeezing, pulling, and twisting, there was almost half an inch of milk in the bucket. I had had enough and my forearms were killing me. I thought, to hell with it, and I gave the cats all the milk and turned the calves in with the cows to finish the job. We'd just have to buy our milk at the store until my brothers could take back over. Rags and I went back to the house to make our report, and the cats deserted us, staying at the barn with the milk. (See? I told you so.) Of course, when my brothers came home that evening, they declared my milking performance a huge success and the job was mine for the next two or three years.

What did I learn from it all? First, that milk bought at the store tastes delicious and it's cheap. Second, milking cows on a daily basis can make you the finest arm wrestler in the fourth grade. Third, after about six months, I became very accustomed to the dark and, indeed, came to like it—a feeling that continues to this day. And last, there are no man-eating tigers in Central Texas. I'm here as living proof of that.

The Quiet Stranger

At Scott School, well over half a century ago, I was the undisputed arm-wrestling champion of the fourth grade. I had been milking our two Jersey cows, Hazel and Cissy, for two years, and any country boy can tell you that the cow-milking business puts power in you forearms, I mean, big time. I stayed in my division and did not venture outside to challenge the fifth graders, but I probably could have whipped them all. At every opportunity, when we had time (and there's a lot of time in the fourth grade), I would issue my challenge to all comers, and after a while, nobody would take me on. No matter. I stayed in training and was prepared to defend my title at the drop of a hat.

One day, we had a new student enter our class, and after a few days, just before we were to take an hour's recess outside, I threw out my normal, and what must have been boring, challenge. To everyone's surprise, the new kid said calmly, "I'll take your challenge."

We all laughed a bit, and I smirked while we set up two desks together so we could sit down on either side. I was shocked that the new kid, who was tall, quiet, and slim, would take me on. The stranger's arms were long, but not heavily muscled at all, and I could not imagine that this would be more than a few seconds' work.

We sat down and put our elbows together and then locked hands. The whole class was watching, and even our teacher, Miss Kreitz, who was never too impressed with our feats of daring-do, seemed to be more interested than usual.

Someone gave the signal, Ready, set—go!" and I instantly put every ounce of my considerable fourth-grade power into my attempt to pin the stranger's hand.

Well, I'm here to tell you that nothing happened. The stranger's arm did not budge an inch. I looked up into my opponent's face, and her gray eyes were smiling and very friendly. She didn't even seem to be trying. Maybe she wasn't. But back in those days, chivalry was alive and well in Central Texas, and she did not pin me in front of all our classmates. She only refused to let me beat her. A gentlewoman she was. I was very impressed at that time and still am.

She was terrific. I gave up and looked over our hands as we relaxed our grip, but we continued to hold hands with our elbows still resting on the desktop.

"You've been milking cows, haven't you?" I said.

She smiled and nodded.

"How many?"

"Three," she said.

"Every day?"

She nodded again.

"That's not fair. I milk only two."

She shrugged.

Well, you can't win them all, and I could not have lost to a better opponent. Empirical knowledge gained in the fourth grade has stood me well for the last half century, and to this day, I'm always careful when dealing with tall, quiet, gray-eyed strangers.

Old Paint

During the summer months, I rolled out of bed every morning except Sunday at an hour before daylight. My mother, God bless her soul, would already be up, preparing a substantial breakfast that would hold me until lunch, for which she would make a couple of sandwiches and add something sweet, like some homemade vanilla cookies with a few M&M's on the side.

Thirty minutes after getting up, I would leave the house, climb in my green '51 Chevrolet, and drive to the E.D. Cook farm, located on river bottom land six miles south of Rogers. The farm had three hundred huge pecan trees and fields of maize, corn, and cotton, the sight of which would make your mouth water. It was a beautiful farm, and one of the reasons it was beautiful was because it was my job to pull the johnsongrass out of every field. It was backbreaking work, and in the ten-acre maize patch, where I toiled all one summer, the maize stood four or five feet tall and the grass was sometimes taller. I pulled the grass while on my knees (It was too hard to pull from a standing position), and the maize and grass covered me up from everything except the sun.

God, it was hot! Ninety-eight degrees in the shade and twenty-five degrees hotter in the sun. I took a thermometer with me one day and checked it out. I worked alone, although the tenant worker, Gene, was on the place; he was always busy doing something else. Besides, he was too smart to pull grass. I was a stupid sixteen at the time and was getting in shape for football season. After pulling grass all summer, Texas high school football was like taking a leisurely stroll with Rebecca at Sunnybrook Farm.

One morning at about 10:30, I heard Gene's old pickup bouncing my way. I got to my feet and walked over to see what he wanted and take a quick drink of water. There were no such things as breaks on the Cook farm.

Gene didn't get out but leaned through the window and said, "Boss wants you to move them heifers to the barn."

"Which ones?" I asked.

"They're in that pasture just below the barn, and I reckon they'll be underneath them trees close to the river."

"All right," I said.

"Git in and you can ride back with me."

I climbed in and rode in the pickup, thankful for the rest.

Gene pulled up to the barn and pointed. "There they are. Just put them in this lot right here."

I got out and surveyed the situation. The field was sixty acres or so, and there looked to be ten or twelve heifers at the far end. I figured I could walk down slowly, get behind them, and ease them up to the barn. Of course, if they did not want to come to the barn, well, a man on foot without a horse or dog would be helpless.

I walked down about two hundred yards and headed them back toward the barn. I didn't shout or make any quick gestures with my arms, and all twelve of them formed a relatively tight group and walked up the gentle hill. Everything went well until I got them to the open gate, which by all rights they should have walked straight on through. The gate was about fifteen or twenty feet wide and strategically located in the corner of the field with the barbed-wire fence around the field, forming a 90-degree funnel that should have been very helpful in encouraging the heifers to go through the gate and into the barn lot. The heifers stopped about fifteen feet before the wide-open gate and refused to go any farther. Why? I have no idea, but something made them nervous. Perhaps they saw a pack of wolves or a wild, rabid rhinoceros, or whatever, so I raised my arms slowly and spoke in my calmest tone, urging them to walk through the gate.

"Come on, girls. Keep walking just a few more feet."

A couple of them snorted and shook their heads and stomped their feet, and I knew that I had lost them. I moved so close that I could almost touch the ones at the back of the pack, and suddenly they all bolted around me in the blink of an eye.

They kicked up quite a bit of dust as they fled back down to the trees along the riverbank, and I wiped the sweat and grit from my eyes and face and walked calmly back to fetch them again. I wasn't overly upset because I knew they were heifers and didn't have any sense, and I would just have to be patient.

And so, again I trudged back down to the tree-lined river and started the heifers off toward the barn, just like the first time. The second trip was a repeat of the first. They moved easily enough back to the open gate, but stalled again, fifteen feet before the entrance. This time, I didn't give them a chance to discuss it all among themselves and shouted and clapped my hands loudly to startle them and, I hoped, get them through the gate before they had time to think about it. Nope. They wheeled about in an instant, even faster then the first time, and scattered like quail, tails high in the air with clinched teeth and forty-eight hooves churning the dust, and I was certain some of them were grinning as they roared past.

I stood there as the dust settled, most of it on me, and considered my options. I didn't really know what to do, but I was not calm anymore and what I really wanted to do was go to the house, get a shotgun, and shoot them. I turned back toward the barn to wash up a bit at the watering trough, and as I did, I looked up and stared straight into the eyes of Old Paint, the boss's mixed Palomino gelding who had been observing all my endeavors from the vantage point of his personal lot. As usual, his front hooves were propped up on the second fence rail (an old railroad tie we had put in 'specially for him because he kept tearing up the regular boards), and his calm, quiet look said to me as plain as day, "I think you need some help, boy."

Now, Paint was smart. He could open any gate or door in the barn, and once he even opened the front door of Gene's house and walked right in. Gene had a big front door. That time he stopped in the living room and really wanted to go back outside, but the room was too small and he couldn't turn around. We pushed him down the short hallway, through the kitchen, and out the screen door on the back porch. After that, we called him a one-way house-horse. As far as I know, that was his only visit inside the house, and Gene's house remains one of the few with hoof marks in the hall. But I digress.

The best thing about Old Paint was you didn't have to saddle up and ride him. He knew what to do. I marched quickly to the gate and slid back the bolt (which was located on the outside so Paint couldn't get to it when he was penned up. He could get in when he wanted, but not out), and then I turned him loose. Paint left the lot and trotted through the barnyard at a hard pace that already shook the ground, and then he broke into an authoritative gallop as he as he passed through the open gate and made straight for the unsuspecting heifers, who were completely unaware that their ways of folly were about to be met with twelve hundred pounds of very direct and righteous retribution. Old Paint was splendid. "Go get 'em, Paint!" I shouted, as he thundered by.

Paint made a beeline for the heifers, who were taken completely by surprise, and only raised their heads to look when Paint was about thirty yards away—much too late. Paint smashed right into the middle of them, slashing right and left, and bit a couple of them who moved too slowly. Those heifers tore out of there at twice the speed in which they had left me standing at the gate, I was still standing at the gate, by the way. They headed back to the barn with bellies low to the ground, legs stretched to the utmost, and tails not quite as high in the air as when they were dealing with me. They got to the gate in record time and nearly ripped the fence down trying not to be the last one through. I had stepped back a safe distance and shouted, "Take that! You Goddamned, balky-bitch heifers!"

I had a perfect view of their frantic, frontal approach, which was in a relatively even horizontal line with Paint hard on their tails. It reminded me of the Remington painting I had seen up in Fort Worth that time, with some Texas Rangers, or cowboys, riding hell-for-leather to escape a bunch of screaming Comanche warriors who were hot on their tails. Old Paint was not as deadly as those Comanches, but the heifers didn't know that. It was a great scene. Those heifers couldn't wait to get through that gate now, and they lunged for the safety of the far corner of the barn lot.

I penned up the heifers and latched the gate. Paint did not follow them in. Paint was tough, but he wasn't mean. Those heifers were now where they were supposed to be, and his job was done. Paint remained free in the main barnyard, and I got some extra-fine feed for him and put it in his favorite bucket, which I placed in the middle of his personal corral. He'd eat it when he was ready, and I left his gate open so he wouldn't have to open it himself when he wanted to go back inside.

"Thanks, Paint," I said, and I gave him a couple of friendly pats on his neck before I left.

Gene and his pickup were nowhere to be found, so I started walking back to the ten-acre maize patch to continue pulling grass. It was very hot, and at every step my boots kicked up the powdery dust into foot-tall clouds that hung suspended above the road and gently marked my passage back down to the river bottom.

The Sprinter

The first track-and-field meet I ever experienced took place in Killeen, Texas, when I was a sophomore in high school. I was not a very good runner, but I was required to participate in the track program because I had every intention of becoming a starter on the football A-team, and running track was part of the deal. My main event was the 880-yard dash, with the last word of that title to be taken with a large grain of salt.

That day, for some reason, after my 880-yard specialty, the coach informed me that all the teams involved were putting together an informal 440-yard relay race and he told me to get ready. I was to run first—start out of the blocks. I said fine, although both the coach and I knew I did not have the speed to do well at 110 yards, but at least the distance was short and I knew I could do my best, even though I had already competed in the 880. I don't remember who my running mates were, but for sure, they were faster than I.

I walked out on the track to loosen up and, to my great dismay, saw that the other three runners off the blocks were black. Now, in those days there were no black students at Temple High School, but it was common knowledge that the black guys were fast as hell, played great basketball, and were hard to tackle in football. The Killeen schools were integrated because Ft. Hood, the largest Army reservation in the US, surrounded Killeen and poured tons of money into the city's economy, and did not put up with that segregation bullshit. Unfortunately, on that day, I was to be an innocent victim of forced integration in Central Texas.

Our manager hammered in the blocks and helped me adjust them to make me comfortable and to ensure I got the best possible start. The black guys did the same. I got in the blocks and arranged the baton in my right hand and put my fingers on the starting line. "On your mark! Get set!" the starter cried. "BAM!" went the pistol, and I took off. Now, if I do say so myself, off the blocks, and in any other running endeavor, for ten to fifteen yards, I am very fast. But after that, I start eating dust.

On that day, before I made three strides, the pistol fired again, indicating a false start and that everyone should stop and go back to the blocks for a restart. And everyone did—except me. As I said earlier, I'd never seen a track meet before, and no one had bothered to tell me all the rules an' such, and I just kept on churning. I could not believe that those black guys had not passed me after fifteen or twenty yards. The wind was roaring in my ears, and I could not believe how well I was doing. *My God, you're terrific!* I thought. I obviously had had some unseen, unknown talent that was making itself manifest at that very moment. It was glorious!

The euphoric feeling lasted until I was rounding the first curve and prepared to hand the baton off to my partner, who was to run the second leg. I looked for him to be crouched down in my lane looking back towards me in order to take off at the precise instant I was the proper distance away. However, he was not ready; he was not even on his feet. He was sitting on the track, holding his stomach with both hands and laughing so hard I could hear him above the roaring in my ears, which was diminishing quickly as I realized that some horrible mistake had been made. I slowed to a walk, stopped, and turned around. I had run a hundred yards completely alone. I was not a fabulous talent that had suddenly, miraculously been discovered. I was a goat. A laughingstock. It was awful. I looked up in the stands, and every eye was looking at me and smiling. Every eye looked like one of those sideways one-eyed portraits painted by Picasso or Braque during the first decade of that century and every face had one grotesque eye that merged with the other, and every face had a huge, silent grin. I have never seen so many teeth in all my life.

There was nothing to do but walk back to the starting line and do it again. I took my time and I don't remember if anyone spoke to me or not. Needless to say, I finished a distant fourth when we finally ran the race. The black guys passed me at about fifteen or twenty yards, just as I had expected them to do the first time, and I guess we finished last in the race—I don't remember. My coach thought the entire incident hilarious, and I wanted to choke him.

I will say that I learned my lesson well and never made that mistake again, nor in the past fifty years have I ever seen my feat duplicated. Indeed, it must still stand as a unique experience in the annals and lore of Central Texas Track and Field.

Panda

In the winter months, when the grazing was sparse, in late afternoons the goats would come down off the high pastures and gather 'round the barn, and I'd go out and feed them shelled corn. We kept the corn in a large bin in the tractor garage. The ground around the garage was worn hard and smooth by the hooves of three hundred fifty goats and very little grass ever grew there, even in spring and summer. The hard ground was perfect for feeding the goats the shelled corn, because not one kernel was ever lost. I would take buckets of corn from the bin and scatter it over half an acre, and they would eat enough to supplement what they could rustle on their own out in the pastures. Feeding the livestock in the cold months was always a pleasure for me, and I would wait outside until dark while they finished eating everything I had brought out.

One day, when I had scattered enough corn on the ground for them all, an old pickup, unknown to me, came rattling up my driveway and pulled to a stop between me and the house, and two fellows got out and walked over.

"Howdy."

"Howdy."

"Where's your dog?" one asked.

"I don't have a dog."

"You've got all those goats and no dog?"

"That's right."

"Come over here." He motioned me around to the back of his pickup. "I've got just what you need."

I walked over to the pickup and looked in the bed. There, wrapped up in a dirty blanket, was a black-and-white Border Collie ball of fur, about the size of an eight-pound bowling ball. If one looked closely, the ball of fur had two sharp little ears, black eyes, and a black nose. The man picked her up and held her high for me to look at.

"This is what you need!" he said grandly. "Five bucks."

He was right. The pup was exactly what I needed, and I reached for my wallet and handed the man a five spot. (Those were the days when I had easy money—not like now.) He gave me the pup, and I took her out into the middle of the herd and gently put her down. I left her there, walked off a ways, turned around, and waited to see what would happen. My goats hated dogs. Well, I'm here to tell you that the goats made a circle with a diameter of about fifteen feet all around her and remained at a respectful distance. She just sat there on her haunches and didn't move, but she was very alert and very cute. If one of the goats, whose weight was at least forty times her own, got too close to her, she would jump toward it and give a tiny bark, or bite on the goat's back leg, and that goat would get out of her way in a hurry, showing her the utmost consideration. I couldn't believe it. Hell, I still don't believe it!

The Mexican guys smiled and laughed, and I was afraid they were going to ask for more money, seeing how she was such a natural. Heck, she couldn't have been more than six weeks old and had surely never seen a goat.

That was the beginning of a strange relationship. I named her Panda and we became caretakers of the goatherd. From the outset, it was strictly a business partnership. She was a bitch in every sense of the word and was never particularly friendly to me, but she took care of the goats, and they loved her. That was the main thing. She never came into the house, never rode in the pickup, and never left the ranch as best I can remember. Together, she and the Little Mare could move the entire herd from one pasture to another or across the farm to market road to the pastures on the other side. They both knew what to do, and all I had to do was stay in the saddle.

Every couple of days, I would ride back into the hills and valleys, checking the top forty for goats that had gotten themselves caught in the vines and brambles. It was always in the late afternoon, and I would call them from the mountaintop, and if a little one was caught in the briars and couldn't get loose, it would call back. I would ride toward the sound, calling again from time to time, and it would answer back until I got close. Then instinct would set in and the goat would cease to answer when it realized something was hunting it. When it would stop calling, I knew I was close. I always found them, but sometimes it took a while. When Panda joined me, the goats would call for help until she was within three feet of them. They were overjoyed when she found them. They weren't too hot about my finding them. Oh well, that was the job she was bred to do, two hundred years before I was born.

I am embarrassed to say I don't know what became of her. After about a year and a half, she just disappeared. She wasn't the first, and she wasn't the last. Life was tough out in those limestone plateaus in Bosque Country, and packs of coyotes, large hawks, wild dogs, and an occasional wolf passed through our territory from time to time. Small dogs, like Panda, didn't last long when they were allowed to run free. I must have had forty or fifty dogs in the first twenty years of my life, most of them just passing through. But she, along with three others, stopped to stay for a while and became a part of my life forever.

The Little Mare

My dad bought a small ranch over in Bosque County, and I moved up there just before my senior year in high school. Nobody was particularly grieved that I left home at the tender age of seventeen. I had a car, some money in my pocket, and a hard-headed attitude that comes with being almost eighteen and being almost always right about almost everything. The place had an old, two-story, four-bedroom frame house on it, and I moved in and set up shop. It was ten miles from Clifton, the nearest town, and at night I could see the seven or eight faint lights of Cranfills Gap, a small hamlet about the same distance away as Clifton, but up the shallow valley in the opposite direction.

Across the road that ran by the front of the house, there was a ninety-acre pasture where we were to grow oats and hay for the livestock. The rest of the property was very rough terrain with modest limestone plateaus, very rocky, with several small gulleys and valleys that were often choked with heavy cedar brakes. It was perfect for goats, and we raised about three hundred fifty Angoras and had fifteen or twenty hearty grade cows and a young, tough Charolais bull. It was a one-man operation that I oversaw with great pride and pleasure, and I took care of it all and went to school, passed my courses (even chemistry), and graduated in the following spring.

Sometime in late September, my dad drove up in a pickup pulling a horse trailer with a horse inside. "I thought you needed a horse up here," he said, and he was right. "Unload her." Looking through the slats as I walked to the back of the trailer, I could see her ribs sticking out and that she looked very tired. I opened the door and as I backed her out, she hit the ground with tiny, dainty feet that would have made a ballerina proud, and I knew that the old man had picked a winner.

I put her in the small lot behind the house for a couple of days so that I could feed her well and we could get to know each other. When she filled out after a month or so, she weighed about nine hundred fifty pounds and had the barrel chest of a typical Texas quarter horse. She had a nice personality and liked me well enough. She was an excellent cow pony but was not so stuffy that she wouldn't work goats as well. Even after fattening up, she was still very light on her feet, and I could not have asked for a better horse and country companion. I called her the Little Mare, and she was a dandy.

In wintertime, on the coldest days, come late afternoon I would saddle up the Little Mare and ride down to my elderly neighbors' house about a mile and a half below my own place. The old man and his wife lived in an ancient frame house, more porous than my own, and they heated their place with a couple of wood stoves. There was no electricity that I ever noted, although an electric line looped down from the farm road. I don't know why they used old-fashioned oil lamps instead of electricity, and I never asked. None of my business. Anyway, I'd pull up close to their front yard between the barn and house and leave the Little Mare with her reins on the ground so she could move around a bit. No cow horse will walk off and leave its cowboy companion afoot to make it back to the house. At least she never did. I don't know who taught her that, but she didn't learn it from me. She had good manners. The old man, who was always outside to feed his cows before dark, would wave me over and I'd give him a hand with the feeding and take a section of a hay bale over to the Little Mare to munch on while I was being neighborly.

After we got the livestock fed, I'd go over to the wood pile and saw up a few logs into splitting-size firewood. Some of the thicker logs I'd go ahead and split up myself and carry a goodly portion over to his porch by the front door, so he could get them whenever he liked, even with his boots off. I didn't overdo it. I'd hang around and help out about forty-five minutes or an hour and then mount up and ride back. Just before leaving, when I walked back to the Little Mare, we'd have the same parting conversation. Every time.

"Sure is a nice little pony you got there," he would say.

"Yes, sir. She sure is."

"She's a dandy."

"Yes, sir." (I had good manners, too. Learned them from the Little Mare.)

"You know old Kleinfelder, over there near the Gap?" he'd ask.

"No, sir. I've heard the name, but don't know him."

"You know what? You know that stud horse he's got? Some feller from Fort Worth drove by his place the other day and offered him five thousand dollars for that stud horse, and old Kleinfelder wouldn't take it! You know what I think?" he asked, getting excited.

"No, sir, I sure don't," I'd answer.

"Well, I figure that's when two fools met!" he would shout, and spit on the ground in disgust.

Then he'd laugh a bit and I would ride out, due north and into the wind.

Once, my other neighbor on the East Side asked me why I always rode down there and left my new '63 Ford pickup at the house.

"Well, it's not that kind of a visit," I replied. "Besides, if I went down there in a new pickup and left the Little Mare at home, he probably wouldn't know who I was, and I know I wouldn't be as welcome. He might even take a shot at me."

I only rode down in the winter months. I figured he didn't need me in the fair weather. I was a foul-weather friend, you might say.

The next fall, I entered Baylor University, in Waco, and made it back to the ranch only on weekends. On one particularly cold day in January or February, I saddled up the Little Mare and with light ice and snow pelting us on our backsides, we went down to check on our neighbors. I could tell from two hundred yards that we were too late. Nothing moved as we stopped at our customary place in the area between the barns and house. No livestock. The place was deserted except for a couple of cats who stuck their heads out from the hayloft door to check us out. I dismounted and left the Little Mare where I always had, and stepped up on the front porch and knocked loudly on the door.

"Hello, the house!" I shouted.

Nothing. I didn't try the door. I turned and walked over to the nearest corral fence and leaned with my forearms on the top rail and propped my foot up on the bottom one. To my right, under the lean-to attached to the barn, there was some leftover firewood for the stoves and the heavy crosscut saw was still hanging on the wall. I felt uncomfortable. I was trespassing, so I walked back to my horse and swung up. It was getting dark and I could tell the Little Mare was getting chilled and was glad to be moving out.

You know what? Five thousand bucks *is* a lot of money—offered, and refused. And he was right. That *was* when two fools met.

Aunt Myrtle

My wife's Aunt Myrtle was probably the richest person in McClennan County. I'm not sure where the money came from—East Texas oil, I think—but wherever it was, there was plenty of it.

She once invited my friend Ramsey (a great squirrel hunter from Indiana) and me out for lunch. We readily accepted and agreed to meet her at a local cafeteria. Although she offered to pick us up, we declined. Ramsey and I sometimes did foolhardy things, but riding in a car with Aunt Myrtle at the wheel was an experience that was well below the line of anything we were willing to risk.

Aunt Myrtle was about eighty-five years old, a little bit senile, and nobody pushed her around. She drove a 1964 golden-brown Oldsmobile with an engine the size of a concert grand piano. With a blade mounted on the front bumper, the car would have made a great snow plow. On the other hand, it probably wouldn't need the blade.

I don't remember which cafeteria we went to or what we ate for lunch, but the events that took place afterward are as clear in my mind as if they had happened yesterday.

After lunch, we followed Aunt Myrtle to her favorite service station, where she filled her car with gasoline. Ramsey and I stopped behind her at what we thought was a safe distance, got out, and helped check the oil and put fresh air in the tires. (She was like that.) When Aunt Myrtle had paid her bill, Ramsey and I started back to our car but halted in mid-stride as Aunt Myrtle gunned the powerful engine and the car exploded out of the service station drive.

The tires screamed furiously and black smoke belched out from behind, as Aunt Myrtle, with hands fixed to the steering wheel and arms locked in a fashion not unlike that of Barney Oldfield, raced out into the street. The car headed straight for the island curb that divided the avenue and when the front wheels made contact, the huge car shot straight up into the air, made a quarter turn, and landed smack in the middle of the lane on the other side. Aunt Myrtle, who could hardly see over the dash, kept the accelerator on the floor and the car leapt forward as soon as the tires hit the pavement again.

With a loud roar, the car smoked its way down the road about sixty feet and, for some inexplicable reason, made a 180-degree turn back over the median and lunged full speed ahead back in the direction of the service station. Ramsey and I had observed the whole scene from the driveway, and we sprang for cover when she headed back our way. We had no reason to worry, however, because when she pulled even with the station, she made another 90-degree turn over the curb and took dead aim on the Dunkin' Donuts store across the street. Now, the Dunkin' Donuts customers had plenty of reason to worry.

In those days, the Dunkin' Donuts buildings were made mostly of glass, especially in the eating area. (They're probably made out of reinforced concrete now.) But because of the excellent visibility from the dining room and because Aunt Myrtle had taken a spectacular warm-up lap before she lined out for the final plunge, the customers were not taken by surprise.

They watched in open-mouthed horror as the car smashed through a row of mail boxes, picked up speed, and headed straight for them. You've never seen folks move so fast in all your life. Two or three people ran into the kitchen, but most made flying leaps over the counter and took refuge between it and the interior wall.

Aunt Myrtle and the Oldsmobile destroyed the Dunkin' Donuts shop. With a gigantic crash, the car smashed through the glass walls and came to a stop about a foot from the counter. Somehow, the car was knocked out of gear, because when Ramsey and I had recovered enough to run across the street, Aunt Myrtle still had the engine racing. The noise was incredible. I reached through the window and cut off the engine.

"Godalmighty!" Ramsey exclaimed. "That's one hell of a car! Look at all those donuts!"

There were donuts everywhere. Ramsey picked up three or four and slipped them over the radio antenna of Aunt Myrtle's car. I don't know why he did that. Battle decorations, maybe. We pried Aunt Myrtle's hands from the steering wheel, and got her out of the car and safely out of the building. It was amazing that not one person was injured in the accident.

Shortly after everyone was outside, I heard the building give a massive sigh and watched as it collapsed in a heap of flattened metal, broken glass, and scrambled donuts. The building was nothing but rubble. When Aunt Myrtle did a job—she did it right!

Texas Showdown—Deuces Wild

My friend Ramsey, a university pal of mine and one of the finest squirrel hunters Indiana ever produced, and I were visiting at my mother's house one beautiful afternoon in late September. We were sitting in Mom's backyard drinking beer under a splendid pecan tree that offered shade from the Central Texas heat, excellent wood for outside grilling, and delicious fruit that, in good years, would melt in your mouth. That tree's worth transcended the mere value of dollars and cents. It was a part of the family. The best part, perhaps.

Our pleasant rest and relaxation was interrupted when Mom stepped out on the back porch and called to us that her longtime friend and confidant, Loyce, needed some help at her place. There was a wild animal of some sort, running loose and wreaking havoc inside her house, and she didn't know what to do about it.

"What kind of animal?" I asked as we got up from our chairs.

"She didn't say, but she sounded very worried and wanted you to come over as soon as possible."

"Call her and tell her we're on our way," I said.

Loyce had definitely called the right people, especially after we'd consumed a couple of beers.

This was several years before the movie *Ghostbusters* was released, but the urgency and potential high drama of the situation would have been perfect for the film. But this was no ghost. It was real. Had Ramsey and I starred in the movie, they probably would have called it *Sodbusters,* but I'm already digressing again, and I'm still on the first page.

Wild animals or no, we didn't think we needed to take a firearm with us. Loyce lived in town, and surely there was no bear or mountain lion loose in her house, and anything else we could probably handle with a stout stick and some loud shouting. Besides, it's bad form to be shooting in the house. Tears hell out of the walls and furniture. We went to the garage and got a hoe handle and a broom, threw them in the back of the pickup as we climbed in and, with all dispatch, took off for Loyce's.

We pulled up in front of her house, grabbed our weapons from the back, and marched to the front porch and rang the doorbell. Loyce opened the door immediately and stared out at us through the screen door. We stood at attention with arms at parade rest and reported for duty. Loyce chuckled and commented that she had not expected such an expeditious response to her call for help and that she was very happy to see us. "Please come in," she said, and held the door open. Ramsey and I trooped in and waited in the living room just inside the front door. We were relaxed and having a good time but were ready for any emergency or sudden attack. "It's in the bathroom," she explained. "I've got the door locked from the outside. Here's the key."

I took the key and walked down the narrow hall to the locked bathroom door, and Ramsey followed along behind with the broom. I had left the hoe handle in the living room because it was too long to be of much use in such close quarters. I wasn't sure how much use the broom would be either, but it was shorter than the hoe handle. Ramsey was six feet four and took up a lot of room with or without a broom. It was going to be interesting. I knew the bathroom was very small and two large fellows, armed with sticks and brooms, and a wild varmint of unknown size and disposition all crammed into one small room at the same time was a recipe for bedlam and disaster.

I squatted down to look through the keyhole in the lock but could see nothing out of the ordinary. I slipped the key into the lock and turned it gently. It made a clicking noise, but I could hear no reaction from inside. I nodded to Ramsey to be ready, and I squatted back down and slowly opened the door. It swung to the inside and bumped gently against the wall. With the door fully open, I could see that the toilet lid had been taped shut, and Loyce had placed five or six heavy encyclopedias (Compton's, I believe they were) on top of the taped-down toilet lid. I assumed the wild animal was inside, and I hoped it was tall enough to keep its head above the water. Well, there was nothing left to do but take off the books and tape and raise the lid. I figured it was a large rat, a snake perhaps, but other than that, I could not imagine what type of critter it might be.

I made sure Ramsey was inside the door as close as possible. He stood in the door frame at the ready immediately behind me, because the room was not big enough for both of us to be in there at the same time. I was on my knees next to the toilet and would keep my head down as low as possible, leaving Ramsey free to subdue the animal with the broom. That was my plan, anyway. If it was a snake and slithered over the toilet bowl lip and onto the floor between my legs and…well, whatever, I wasn't real sure just what we'd do. And snakes are fast, too, let me tell you! We'd just have to wing it—play it by ear.

I removed the Compton's and reached around the door frame to put them out in the hall. Then I started pulling off the tape. How Loyce had coaxed the varmint into the toilet, I had no idea, but once inside she had made damn sure it was going to stay there. There was a lot of tape. Finally, I came to the last strand and looked up at Ramsey to make sure he was ready and still focused.

He nodded grimly and the moment had arrived. I took off the last of the tape, and nothing happened. I started to lift the lid, and bam!, a furry creature exploded out of the toilet like a shot from a canon. Water flew everywhere, and the creature jumped for the top of the medicine/shaving cabinet on the opposite wall. With a loud shout, Ramsey took a mighty swing at it and aimed a little low and hit me in the back of the head, knocking me flat on my back on the bathroom floor, where I remained for the duration of the entire struggle, about fifteen seconds or so. Ramsey swung again at the squirrel (for that's what it was), and it ran around the wall to the other side of the bathroom, hopping and dodging, and my view from the bathroom floor was fantastic. Ramsey, with clenched teeth and blazing eyes, swinging that broom like Ted Williams at the plate (but unlike Ted, he never connected—with the squirrel, that is) and the squirrel's successfully eluding his every swing. Finally, the squirrel made a mistake and fell into the clothes hamper in the corner. Ramsey quickly grabbed the top, which had been knocked off in the fracas, slammed it shut, and we had him. I checked to make sure that Ramsey had finished swinging and then got up off the floor.

"Damn! You were terrific, Ramsey!" I exclaimed.

"Yeah, well, we got the little bugger."

We picked up the laundry basket and dumped the entire contents outside through the small open window on the west wall. The window had no screen, and the squirrel had probably come inside looking for a drink of water and fell in. I bet he never did that again.

Loyce, who had been listening to all this from the safety of her kitchen, came down the hall and cautiously stuck her head around the corner of the door.

"What was it? Did you get it? Anybody hurt?"

"Yes, ma'am," Ramsey said. "It was just a little ol' squirrel, and we tossed him out the window with some of your clothes. Everybody's fine."

"My goodness. This place is a disaster. Hard to believe just one squirrel could cause such a mess."

"Yes, ma'am, they're always a mess when they come in the house. They're a nuisance." Ramsey knew about such things.

"Well, you gentlemen have done a fine job and you can go home now. I can clean all this up by myself."

"Yes, ma'am."

I picked up my hoe handle in the living room, and we walked outside to the pickup.

"Thank you," she called from the porch.

"You're welcome, Loyce. Anytime," I said.

We got in and I cranked the engine. "Man, I had a good time!"

"Me too," said Ramsey, "but I think my beer got warm out there on your mom's table."

"Well, we can fix that. Let's stop by Strasburger's and pick up some more. I worked up a powerful thirst lying there on the bathroom floor."

"Yeah, but I did all the hard work and I think it's your turn to buy."

"No question about it," I agreed, and we picked up a cold six-pack and headed back to our former post at Mom's house, under the shade of the finest pecan tree in Temple, Texas.

Yellow Thunder!

Waco, Texas, is the home of Baylor University, an institution I managed to graduate from in the late summer of 1969. It was a year and a summer later than I was scheduled to graduate, but I was not in a hurry to get educated and then go immediately to Vietnam, where I was sure to get my ass shot off. There are some things you just don't have to do in a hurry.

My family owned a huge white house on Speight Street, just south of the University campus, and I shared large, beautiful second-story room and bath with my good friend, Ramsey, a great squirrel hunter from Indiana. Ramsey was tall (about six feet four) and thin, spoke with a slow drawl, wore cowboy boots and hat, and looked and acted more Texan than I. However, there was one characteristic he possessed that separated him from anyone I have ever met, before or since. He slept with his eyes open. When he went to sleep, his eyes rolled back (upward, I presume) in his head and the irises simply disappeared. His eyelids stayed completely open and all you could see were, literally, the whites of his eyes. At first, it was a little scary to be in the same room with him at night, but after a while I got used to it. They didn't shine in the dark, thank God, but it was still just a little bit spooky.

One night, I came in late and Ramsey was already asleep. I took off all my clothes and walked over across the room to crawl in my bed, close to the bay windows on the south wall. The night passed without incident and I awoke early, just before sunup. I got out of bed and walked back across the room to put on my clothes, which I had left next to the door the night before. As I walked across the room, I noticed Ramsey, sound asleep, staring out into the Great White Vast Unknown. No problem, and I reached for my underwear, which I had left hanging on the door handle.

Now, in those days, Waco was not the cosmopolitan city it has become today. Perhaps hotel accommodations were scarce that night, I don't know. But somehow, for some reason, five yellow jackets (we counted their remains later) decided to spend the night in my brand-new jockey briefs. Unsuspectingly, I took my underwear off the door handle, slipped them on and pulled them up snug and tight, and it made those yellow jackets mad as hell!

Bam! Wham! They started blasting away at close range with all the potent firepower they possessed. With a loud whoop, I leapt into the air and almost banged my head on the ceiling. As I came back down to the floor, I started whaling away at those yellow jackets with my right hand, slapping myself on the most private, personal, and important parts of my body. I was shouting and jumping all over the room, and Ramsey was wide awake. You should have seen the look on his face. He couldn't imagine what was happening and after his initial shock and rude awaking, he started laughing so hard that he fell out of bed. In the meantime, I slacked off on my almost brutal attempts to kill the yellow jackets; there was a fine line between killing them and doing myself some permanent harm. After a couple of what must have been spectacular trips around the room, I got the hang of it and managed to slow down enough to get my underwear off and check the damage. It was considerable.

The yellow jackets had met a grim demise, but they had put up a short and vicious fight. You couldn't blame them, really. I would not have wanted to be awakened like that either. My new underwear was completely destroyed by about four seconds of extremely severe wear. Ramsey did not injure himself when he fell out of bed and I recovered quickly, although I did walk a little funny until sometime past noon. All things considered, it could have been worse, and I was grateful to have survived the encounter with the yellow jackets, relatively unscathed.

When the weather permits, I still sleep in the nude, but I am here to tell you that, of a morning, when I put my underwear on, I always check for yellow jackets. I highly recommend that you do the same. Just give your underwear a couple of good shakes before you slip them on. One day you may want to thank me for this sage advice.

Jehovah's Witnesses

It was hot that early afternoon. August-in-Texas hot. I rolled out of my comfortable old reclining chair and stumbled over to answer the knock at the door, opened it, and there they were, standing there in white long-sleeved shirts with earnest looks and dark ties, sweating in the two o'clock sun. I knew who they were. Jehovah's Witnesses. They had to be. Not even Mormons venture out in such heat.

"Can I help you?" I asked pleasantly.

"Yes," the older one replied. (He was in his late twenties.) "We'd like to talk to you about the Bible and how it relates to our world today."

"Gentlemen," I said, "I am honored and I have read the Bible several times, but I simply do not feel qualified to advise you in such an important matter. But my good friend, Ed Cherryholmes, is the pastor of the Methodist Church here in town, and he would be pleased to assist you. He knows a lot about the Bible. He lives right down the street."

How do I think of answers like that?

"No, no," they protested. "We'd like to talk to *you*."

"I understand," I said and continued. "Please come in. It's hot out there. Would you care for a cold beer? I'm sorry that's all I have at the moment, because I drank all the whiskey last night."

They stopped in mid-stride over the threshold and backed up. The finest mule tandem in Bosque County could not have dragged them through the front door.

"No thanks," they said. "We can just talk from here."

They offered me one of their magazines they carry around with them which I took but didn't look at. I waited.

The older one began. "Do you believe in Jesus?" he asked.

"Do you mean did he exist? Well, as a matter of fact, I do. I believe he said and did some very cool things. You know, the sermon on the mound an' all. And he had guts. You've got to hand it to him. He told everybody exactly what he thought. He didn't pull any punches either, no matter who he was talking to. Now, his old man. God, I mean, I could never work up a great deal of respect and admiration for him for several reasons. He had kind of a mean streak, you know? But he did produce a mighty fine boy! Now, what else?"

They shuffled around a bit and said nothing. Collecting their thoughts, I guess.

I looked the older one straight in the eye and said, "It's too hot out here to be hustling converts for the Lord. Now, you take that boy swimming. The San Marcos River is ten minutes south of here, and that spring water is cold and crystal clear. I guarantee you that there are some souls to be saved down at the river. You could baptize them on the spot." Do Jehovah's Witnesses baptize folks? I'll have to ask them the next time.

He nodded in authoritative agreement and the boy—he must have been seventeen or eighteen—nodded a bit more enthusiastically and almost smiled. They were turning around to leave and I had almost shut the door when I thought of one more thing.

"Wait a minute," I said. "Let me share this with you before you go."

All southern fundamentalist Christians cannot resist the word "share."

"You know that prophet, Elisha?"

They both nodded again but got a glazed look over their faces and I knew they didn't know the prophet Elisha from Adam's asshole. It's not really surprising, though, because in my Bible, Adam's asshole and Elisha are separated by about four hundred pages—long pages with small print and no pictures. A substantial distance.

"You remember when he went into that country village and fixed up the drinking water and made it taste sweet again? Well, when he was leaving town, a bunch of those mean boys followed him out on the road, laughing and making fun of him because he was bald-headed. He got pissed off about that and called she-bears down out of the mountains and the bears ate thirty-nine of those boys. That's my favorite Bible story!"

They were falling all over themselves trying to get out of there, but I wasn't finished.

"And by the way, don't bother to knock on my neighbor's door. She's not as nice as I am. She's a retired FBI agent and she's a dead shot with a .38!" And with that, I slammed the door shut.

I watched their backs from the living room window as they slowly walked across the road to the house of the next prospective convert. They seemed to stoop a bit in the heat, and their feet kicked up little puffs of dust as they continued on their earnest, ancient mission. I almost felt sorry for them.

I moved back over to my favorite reclining chair and resumed my former position.

You know what? Those Jehovah's Witnesses were on to something. The Bible does relate to our world today, and it definitely proves one thing for sure. We bald-headed dudes have always had a great sense of humor.

On the Road to El Paso

It was around 4:30 one March afternoon when I left the big city and drove south on Interstate Highway 35 to my home in the small town of Kyle. As I crossed into Hays County, I stopped off at a convenience store to pick up some chips and dips to take to the house. After making my purchases, I left the shopping center area and as I was driving on the access road to get back up on the main highway, I saw an unlikely looking hitchhiker who flagged me down. She was dressed in a thin, ankle-length white skirt and white blouse, and the nippy March winds whipped the lightweight skirt tight against her long, slim legs. She quickly folded her arms across her chest when she realized I was picking her up and hugged herself as she ran the few yards to where I waited for her. She was not dressed for the early spring weather, and it would become colder as the late afternoon waned into evening. She climbed into the passenger side of the big pickup and smiled and said thank you. I greeted her and continued on the access road for about fifty yards until I merged back into the light traffic on the freeway. She was between thirty and thirty-five and good-looking.

"Where are you headed?"

"I'm going to El Paso," she answered quietly.

"Tonight?"

"Yes."

"My dear lady, you are not dressed warmly enough to be out on the highway, and do you know how far it is to El Paso?" At least twenty other questions flooded my thoughts, but I saved them.

She did not respond, but smiled sweetly.

It was about five miles to Kyle, but I had at least thirty miles of questions. I didn't really know where to begin.

"What's your name?"

"Levi," she pronounced it European style, not like the jeans, and I took it to be her family name.

What is a nice, extremely attractive Jewish girl like you doing out here alone, on the side of the highway? I thought, but said, "What do you do, Miss Levi?"

"I'm a painter."

I believed her. She was just a little bit spacey. She had a small shoulder bag, no hat or coat, no plan that made any sense, from what I could tell, and no defense. She was ripe for the taking by any of those predators who travel the big highways, looking for the quick kill. I do not like to mind other folks' business, but if I did not take her matters into my own hands, she would not survive the night.

"I am worried about you," I said. "Where are you going to spend the night? Do you have friends or family around here? It's seven hundred miles to El Paso. (It's at least seven hundred miles to El Paso, I don't care where you start from. It's even farther coming back.) Will you spend the night in San Antonio?" I wanted her to say yes.

She only shrugged. She didn't know. Maybe she didn't care. She didn't seem upset or angry, but she certainly was not thinking straight and was not overly concerned about anything that I was very concerned about.

We pulled off the highway at the Kyle exit, and I took her to the main intersection of the small downtown area. I stopped the pickup and showed her the corner where she should stand and explained, "There's a shelter in San Marcos, where you can spend the night. The people turning right at this corner will be headed toward San Macros, and someone will give you a lift. It's only eight miles south of here, and it's on the road to San Antonio and, eventually, El Paso. You should be able to get a ride easily."

And with that, I ignominiously left her on the street. I was in too much of a hurry to get home, make myself a tall drink, settle down in my comfortable chair, and listen to Alfred Brendel play Schubert. My home was two minutes from where I left her, and no sooner had I stepped through the front door than the alarm bells started to clang loudly in my head and I jumped back in my pickup and high-tailed it back to the intersection to take her to San Marcos myself—something I should have done in the first place. I made it just in time, but barely.

As I drove up, I could see her getting in the back seat of a white two-door car, while one rough-looking fellow held the door for her. There was another guy behind the wheel. I stopped my truck in the middle of the intersection, right in front of their car and, in my haste, left the engine running and the door open as I strode over to the guy standing at the door.

"I want her out of that car, and I mean right now!" I declared. I didn't know how successful my command was going to be, but I did know that I had to get her out. Her life depended on it.

The two men were not as big as I was, but they were big enough and half my age, and my days of whipping two tough guys at the same time had long since passed, if indeed there ever were such days. I would just have to do my best.

To my great surprise and huge relief, the guy outside smiled and said, "No problem, sir. We were just trying to give the lady a hand," and he pulled the front seat forward and did give her a hand out of the car.

I couldn't believe my good fortune and their amiable acquiescence to my blustery order until, out of the corner of my eye, back and to the left, I saw the approaching bulk of Kyle Police Officer John Callaghan. Officer Callaghan was six feet, two inches tall and weighed two hundred seventy pounds. He was a very imposing figure, and the pistol on his hip was a thing of beauty, at least from my perspective.

"You gentlemen got a problem here?" he asked.

No, sir, we sure don't," I said. "Everything's working out here just like it should."

The guys smiled and waved and got the hell out of there. Of course, Officer Callaghan knew something was not right. My pickup was still in the middle of the intersection, and he obviously knew the two cowboys in the white car.

"Those two individuals are trouble," he stated. "Better move your pickup."

I told Miss Levi to wait with Mr. Callaghan while I moved the pickup to the side of the road. I got back out and explained to John what had happened. "There's a shelter in San Marcos, and I'll give her a ride down there."

"That's a good idea," he said. "I'll give them a call and tell them you're coming."

He told me approximately where the shelter was located and said they'd be expecting me. I thanked him and he nodded as he turned away, saying nothing. Routine for him, I guess. I opened the shotgun door for Miss Levi and gave her a boost up onto the seat. She said thanks and I walked around and got in.

Miss Levi appeared to be vaguely aware of what she had narrowly escaped, but her countenance remained serene and mildly happy, although I could tell she wasn't so hot about going to the shelter for the night, but she could not come up with any reasonable alternative. I told her she would be safe at the shelter, it would be warm, and they would give her something to eat. That pitch sounded so good, I almost considered spending the night there myself.

We took the downtown highway exit and I drove around in the area Officer Callaghan had described to me, but I didn't see any likely place. I wasn't sure what a shelter looked like, anyway. I pulled into a gravel parking lot of a rather large, gymnasium-like building and went inside to inquire. I told Miss Levi to wait in the truck and I'd be right back. I took the keys with me.

I went inside and realized immediately it was a dojo, and I saw the black-belted master out on the mats with about fifteen young children in small white ghis, acting like baby goats, bouncing and prancing around under the shepherd's watchful eye. It had been twenty years since I'd been in a dojo, but I had not forgotten my manners. I slipped off my cowboy boots and bowed as I stepped onto the mat to approach the master. I bowed again to him and his students and they bowed to me. I felt very comfortable.

"I am sorry to trouble you," I said, "but I am on a worthy mission and need some help."

"How can I help you?" he asked quietly, He was five feet, nine inches tall, and weighed one hundred eighty pounds. He had a calm, cool look and was one of those guys whose feet whispered across the mat as he came to you and would deposit your raggedy ass in the nickel seats if you were not very careful. I liked him.

"I'm looking for the shelter where needy people can spend the night and get something to eat. It's supposed to be very close to here."

"Go back out the door you came in, and it's on the other side of the parking lot."

"Thank you," I said, and bowed and left the shepherd and his kids.

Miss Levi got out of the pickup and we walked across the parking lot to the shelter. It was a small brown frame house with a porch stretching across the entire front of the building. We climbed the wooden stairs, knocked on the door, and went inside.

We met the young man and his wife, who were the supervisors of the place, and they invited us to sit down and have a cup of coffee. I don't remember their names, but they were very kind and friendly and made Miss Levi and me very welcome. I explained the situation to them and asked to see the accommodations where she would be spending the night. The husband showed me around, and it was clean and cheerful. There were four or five rooms, enough space for eight or ten visitors, although it was still early in the evening and Miss Levi was the only patron for the moment. He and I stepped out on the porch, and I explained in a bit more detail how I came to bring her to the shelter and that she had a plan to go to El Paso, and that I knew nothing more. He understood and said that they could help her for the evening and would see what they could do for her on the morrow. He had been in the situation before, practically every night, and they would be able to be of assistance.

While we had been outside talking, the wife had brought Miss Levi a bowl of stew and she was sitting at the table, eating hungrily as we returned.

"Is it tasty?" I inquired.

"I like it," she said with satisfaction.

Well, thank God! It was the first encouraging, positive thing I'd heard her say. We were both getting happier. I told her I had to be leaving and that the nice couple would take care of her. She nodded, without getting up. I took off my favorite, very old and comfortable, ripped and torn Levis jeans jacket and gave it to her.

"Here, take this. You're going to need it tomorrow."

She remained seated and nodded and smiled her thanks, holding the jacket in her lap. I said goodbye to her and left. The young man followed me out on the porch.

"It's a nice thing you've done. Thanks."

"No problem."

"Do you believe in God?" he asked suddenly.

"Well, I do, but I'm sometimes not too impressed with his handiwork."

He looked at the floor and said nothing.

"Goodbye," I said.

"Goodbye."

I walked across the parking lot, got in my pickup, and drove to the house. On the way back, I thought that if the Big Man was watching over us folks, I hoped he had a few good agents located out there between San Antonio and El Paso, because I knew somebody who was going to need them.

Uncle Edi and the Simmeringer Boys

My immersion into Viennese life and culture was one of the major influences of my education, both professionally and personally. In total, I spent about seven years in Vienna, studying and singing, and my wonderful friends there, American and Austrian, were instrumental in making the experience the most influential and significant of my adult life. Jim and John, my very good American friends, whom I had met in the Seventh Army Soldiers' Chorus in Heidelberg, preceded me to Vienna after our military tours were over, and they had been living there for two years by the time I arrived. They had already established a network of friends and acquaintances, who immediately became my friends and acquaintances, just by showing up.

Several of our best Austrian friends came from Simmering, the Eleventh District of Vienna. They all had been friends since their school days, and Jim and John—and eventually, I—became adopted Simmeringer Boys when we were in their territory. (Hell, I'm still a Simmeringer Boy.) They, their wives and girlfriends, and extended families were nice people. I am especially grateful that all of them tolerated my fumbling, bumbling, and basically boring German for most of my sojourn in their fair city, and they offered nothing but encouragement and compliments as I struggled with their language. I remain most appreciative of their patience and understanding and use their kind, practical examples in teaching my own students English, an equally difficult foreign language.

In those days, our main meeting place in Simmering was at Wolfi's. He and his family had a bookstore on the main street, and the family owned the large building, which housed the bookstore and several apartments. It was a four-story affair with a large enclosed garden in the back, and we spent many hours at Wolfi's house and gardens. When the weather was right, we had outdoor parties with basketball, dancing, and always music-making, with plenty of excellent food and shocking amounts of beer, wine, and schnapps. Although the Americans were the only ones actually studying music and from time to time performing professionally, the Austrians were all very fine musicians, and we put together concerts and performed throughout the city and at many venues in the surrounding countryside.

Wolfi's dad, Mr. Ratz, was a wonderful fellow who asked us to call him Uncle Edi. He was a quiet, unassuming gentleman who never raised his voice or lost his temper, a remarkable achievement considering the large groups of people who were often visiting his property, many of them loudmouthed, rowdy foreigners who (according to his wife) were terrible influences on the local young people. Thinking back on it all now, she wasn't too far off the mark.

Uncle Edi could never get our (the three Americans) names matched up with our faces. It was surely a challenge for him because all our names began with J. All were one-syllable words, all were musicians, all were going bald, all were very outgoing, and all were always hungry. I, myself, get confused just thinking about it now. He finally hit on a foolproof plan and called all of us, collectively and individually, Jimjackjohn. He spoke the new name quickly, it still had only three syllables, and it worked perfectly.

In 1978, I returned to the United States for an extended stay, and Uncle Edi passed away in December of 1979. I got word of his passing from several of the Simmeringer Boys, and it saddened me very much. Since that time, I've been in Vienna on several occasions, and I am embarrassed to say that I have not had the good manners to drop by his final resting place in the Simmeringer Cemetery for a visit and to pay my respects. I did go to the cemetery one time, alone, and could not find it. Uncle Edi was a very patient man, and I know he is aware that, once, I did show up, but was unsuccessful in my search.

Next time, I'll ask Wolfi or the beautiful Christine, his sister—perhaps both—to go with me. We'll light candles and place them on Uncle Edi's gravestone. He'll like that, and I know he is looking forward to our visit.

Tempo rallentando al fine.

"Continue to rest in peace, Uncle Edi," I'll pray.

"And thank you, Uncle Edi," I'll say.

"From yours most truly."

Jimjackjohn

Dropping Names

The first two years I lived in Vienna were tough, mainly because I had no money. I was a pretty good singer and had expected to land a job in a provincial opera house, somewhere in Austria or Germany, but the opera house intendants (artistic directors) were not particularly impressed with my abilities, and after months of failed auditions, I decided to enter the Musikhochschule and study further. It was a necessary decision.

The instruction offered by the Hochschule was excellent and inexpensive, and with the money I received from the Army's GI Bill, I survived—barely. Sometime near the end of my first year of study, one of my teachers, Professor Brandtner, declared to me that I simply did not understand the texts of the songs I was singing with her (Hoelderlin and Fortner) and that there was very little more she could do for me. She was an attractive woman, about six foot two, and weighed a solid one hundred eighty pounds.

"Herr Everton," she fretted. "Here we are, I, a poor, defenseless woman, and you, a big, strong man. And I am working like a poor slave to help you, and you are not holding up your end of the effort. What more can I do?" she sighed.

Defenseless? How, did she get defenseless in there? She was about as defenseless as the Pittsburgh Steelers. I wiped the sweat from my brow and said nothing. Maybe a "yes, ma'am," or something. I had been working like a dog.

"Look," she continued. "In this theater, there are many actors who are performing and rehearsing daily. Go down to the Kantine and ask one of them to help you. I am at my wit's end. Good day, Herr Everton!"

(I could tell she liked me.)

The next day, I was sitting at a table with my friend, Olson, and I noticed a fellow standing at the bar whom I had seen several times recently. I picked up my book and walked over and put it on the counter beside him.

Without preamble, I asked him, "You're an actor, aren't you?"

"Sometimes," he said.

The Kantine became deathly quiet. You could have heard a pin drop.

"My teacher told me to get some help with these poems, and I was wondering if you had a few minutes to give me a hand."

"What poems are they?" he asked without moving.

"Hoelderlin," I said and began to recite the first line.

He held up his hand to stop me. He then proceeded to recite all four poems from memory. He was fantastic, and when he finished, the entire place erupted with enthusiastic applause. I thanked him and went back to my table, where Olson was waiting.

"Do you know who that is!?" He spoke *sotto voce*.

"I have no idea, but he's pretty good."

"Pretty good, hell! That's Josef Meinrad! You just spoke with God in the German-speaking world of theater. Why did you do that, anyway?"

"Professor Brandtner told me to."

"To ask him?"

"Not really. Just anybody," I said.

"Well, you picked the best. Brandtner won't believe it. Did you actually learn anything? It doesn't matter. Just tell her you worked with Josef Meinrad, and she'll think you have improved tremendously."

At my next lesson with Professor Brandtner, I knocked on the door and went in. She got up from the piano and greeted me as if she hadn't seen me in years.

"Herr Everton, I'm so delighted to see you! How are you?"

"Fine, Frau Professor, and I have worked hard on the Hoelderlin poems," and I had, "and I think they're much better now."

"Wonderful!" she said. "And did you get some advice from one of our artists here in the theater?"

"Yes, I did. Josef Meinrad was kind enough to give me some tips."

"Josef Meinrad!" she exclaimed. "My God! He helped *you* with the texts?"

Her emphasis on the "you" was a bit more than I liked, but I had to agree with her.

"He did, and he was very nice about it, too."

"Unbelievable!" she said. "Let's hear them."

I sang much better that day, and she declared that Meinrad was obviously as great a teacher as he was performer, but I didn't tell her that I had worked on the songs with three other distinguished teachers and scholars since I had seen her last. Discretion remains the better part of valor, and sometimes you just don't have to tell the whole truth.

Larry Fuller, a distinguished choreographer and dancer, was also very helpful in my early career in Vienna. During my student days, I got a call from the American Embassy, and the person told me they would like for me to come to audition for a special performance that was to take place in Bucharest in one week's time. They were obviously desperate. They didn't say, but I'm sure their first, second, and third choices had somehow fallen through and they were in a bind. They wanted me to come that afternoon. I agreed, of course, because I was broke and desperate myself. At the audition, I sang well enough, and a pushy woman who was the boss said I would do. The show involved two singers, two dancers, and a pianist, and was being directed by Larry. All the music was from Broadway, not my main field of expertise, but I could fake it and was also able to learn all the music during the coming week—no small feat.

They had engaged an excellent pianist from the Vienna Conservatory, and he and I worked every day throughout that week to get the music in good shape. I met Larry during one of the musical sessions, and he was very polite and unassuming for such a star. He was a nice guy.

We were to drive in a van from Vienna, through Hungary to Bucharest, and we left two days before our performance. A driver came with the van, and early one morning we all piled in and set off.

In those days, it was a substantial undertaking to drive from Vienna to Bucharest. The border guards and police in Hungary and Romania were not very friendly, and we were looked upon with a great deal of suspicion by all (the official people, that is). We did not stop to enjoy the sights, and the trip was strictly business. Nightfall caught us in eastern Hungary, and I will never forget how dark it was in the Hungarian countryside after the sun went down. The farms had no lights, and there were no farm trucks or tractors. Wagons were pulled by oxen or horses. There was no electricity and no gasoline engines, and the overall provincial poverty and complete lack of modernity of any apparent kind was depressing. "Grim" is perhaps a better word.

We passed over the border into Romania, and the two-lane road became more precarious as we drove through mountains that were covered in snow. The narrow road had substantial potholes that would have broken an axle had we fallen in. We drove approximately twenty-five miles an hour and it was not a pleasant journey, especially for our driver. Eventually, we needed to buy gasoline, and there were no dwellings of any kind for miles, much less gasoline stations.

At around 2:00 A.M., we finally stopped in a very small, dark cluster of mountain houses to see if we could find some gasoline. Being the tough, Texas-type guy that I was, I volunteered to venture out in the dark, snow, and cold to find some gas. I knocked on a couple of doors and (polite as hell) inquired about buying some gasoline. Even at that hour, the villagers were very charming and friendly, and one of them had some gasoline in his barn and we bought a five-gallon can's worth from him. I don't remember what it cost, but Larry doubled the asking price. Larry got out of the van to pay the man, and we talked a bit while the villager put the gas in the tank.

"I'm so glad you're on this trip," he said to me.

"Hey, me too!"

"I just want you to know, if there's ever anything I can do for you, be sure and let me know." He was sincere.

"Thanks," I said. "I'll feel free to ask."

"Please do."

We then had enough gasoline to get out of the mountains, and we eventually came to an open service station located on the relatively flat plains, and we filled up and headed for Bucharest.

In that city, our performances went well and were very well received. My singing partner, an excellent and good-looking soprano from Graz, and I sang well, and Larry and his dancing partner, an American ballerina, also engaged in Graz, were terrific. Our hotel was very old and very comfortable. It had only two stories and it completely surrounded a large, Mexican-style patio, which was wonderful but would have been even more so in warm weather. Our short stay in the capital city was very successful and a lot of fun.

I remember very little about our return home, except the exhilarating feeling I got when we crossed over the border from Hungary into Austria and I could see lights in the countryside at night. I thought I had reached the promised land.

About six months later, after I had spent a great deal of time and effort studying in Vienna and auditioning in Austria and several cities in southern Germany, I finally landed a position at the Theater an der Wien, a distinguished theater located a ten-minute walk from my apartment on Mariahilferstrasse. I was hired for the summer production of "The Merry Widow" and would be singing in the chorus—a position I thought somewhat beneath my abilities, but the money was right and I was hungry. I was delighted to have the job.

The first question they asked me after I signed my contract was, "Can you waltz?"

"Well, I waltz okay. I understand three-quarter time."

"I mean Viennese Waltz," the director said.

"Probably not."

"You'll have to learn as soon as possible."

I assured him I would, and we shook hands and I left the theater.

Late that same afternoon, I gave Larry Fuller a call and reminded him who I was, the gas man from Romania, and that I was calling in the marker he had so generously promised. He remembered me and asked what I needed.

"I need to learn how to waltz, Viennese style. I have an engagement at the Theater an der Wien in 'The Merry Widow,' and they said I have to learn the Viennese Waltz."

"Can you waltz at all?" he asked.

"Sure, I dance okay."

"Fine. Just tell them I taught you and that should suffice."

And that was that.

The next week at our first rehearsal, the director asked me if I had learned the Viennese Waltz.

"Yes," I said. "Over the weekend, I got some coaching from Larry Fuller."

"Ach! Herr Fuller!" he exclaimed. "Well, that's wonderful!"

And from then on, I was considered the best waltzer in the entire troupe. Actually, I wasn't the best; there were a couple of fellows who were better than I, but they didn't have the Fuller name behind them. It also didn't hurt that I could keep my feet planted firmly on the floor while dancing do-si-dos with two-hundred-pound sopranos. I never brought it up at the time, but I can tell you that bull-dogging steers and hauling seventy-five-pound hay bales in the hot Texas sun were excellent preparation for being right at home on stage with the Viennese Waltz.

Texas and Tirol

The Kantine in the basement of the Acadamie Theater was the favorite meeting place of the Musikhochschule Vocal Department. The theater itself was a going concern, and there were major theatrical performances there every night. The Musikhochschule used the building throughout the day, and the main stage as well, from time to time. The Kantine was a very busy place, and there were interesting people there at all hours of the day and night, seven days a week.

One afternoon, my lessons were over and I walked in and saw Olson at one of the tables. I wandered over and sat down.

"What are you doing here? I thought you finished an hour or so ago."

"That's right," he said. "Since then, I've been waiting on you so you can buy me a beer."

"Well, I don't mind if I do," I said, and got back up and walked to the counter to order.

The Kantine was self-serve for everybody, no matter how big a star you were.

"Two beers, please," I ordered in German (a genius).

There was a stranger standing next to me at the counter, and he turned to me and asked, "Do you mind if I say something?"

"Not at all," I said cheerfully. "Fire away!"

"You're either from Texas or Tirol," he declared.

I was surprised, and with good reason. I doubt that sentence had ever been uttered before, in any language. Tirolers are free spirits and are considered rather wild and crazy, and we Texans have that reputation, too. (Neither group is as wild and crazy as Oklahomans, but that's another story.) But how did he know that?

"You're exactly right," I told him. "I'm from Texas."

He nodded absentmindedly and said, "I thought so," and turned around and walked off.

The Bully

During the first years of my study at the Musikhochschule, I had a small apartment in the Thirteenth District, not far from the Schoenbrunn Palace. It had a combination bedroom/living room, a very small bath, and a comfortable kitchen with large windows that opened out on the street with the sills about four feet above the sidewalk. It would have been very nice if I'd had enough money to heat the place. It was part of a large apartment complex that consisted of four substantial buildings about fifteen stories tall that were arranged around a large garden or Hof, in which there was a pleasant green lawn and three or four large clotheslines for the tenants to use.

On Saturday or Sunday morning, I would wash my clothes by hand in my small Sitzbad and then take them outside into the garden and hang them out on one of the clotheslines to dry. Most of the time, I would leave them on the line until evening or the following morning.

After a month or so of my residence there, I began to notice an older Viennese woman who was often in the garden when I went out to hang up or bring in my clothes. She would constantly talk under her breath, but loud enough for me to hear, about the dirty foreigners who were ruining the neighborhood and were always leaving their dirty jeans and other clothes on the line, which was intended for apartment owners, not dirty, foreign renters like me. For about six weeks, I tolerated her mutterings and insults and always greeted her in a very friendly and proper fashion. She was, after all, an old woman who was found in every neighborhood, in every city throughout the world. Until one day, she caught me in a bad mood.

I was carrying my clothes to the line that morning, and she was watering the grass with a garden hose about forty feet from me as I hung up my clothes. Maybe she was in a bad mood, too, because she was not mumbling, but speaking quite loudly her usual monologue about dirty foreigners. I left my clothes basket under the clothesline and walked quickly over to where she was watering.

"Now, lady, I'm always very nice and polite to you, but I'm tired of listening to your negative comments about me, and I'm not going to put up with it anymore. I would like to speak with your husband, and I mean right now!"

"I don't have a husband and blah, blah, blah…."

She started shouting very loudly and quickly, and I didn't understand everything she said. It didn't matter, but she was not backing up and was hanging in tough.

I reached down and took the hose away from her and lightly sprayed the left side of her face, not with the full force, but just enough to get the desired effect.

She started jumping up and down and screaming, "You're a bully! You're a bully!"

"That's right, lady," I said in a soft voice, "and the next time I come in this garden, you'd better keep your mouth shut! Do you understand?"

Those last words I spoke to her back because she was already on her way out of the garden and into the building. I dropped the hose down on the grass and went over to the faucet to cut it off. As I turned and walked back to continue hanging out my clothes, seven or eight floors up, a window opened and the old lady leaned out and continued shouting at me and waving her right forefinger in a naughty, naughty sort of way, and as far as I was concerned, there was nothing more to be done about the matter. The water from the hose would not reach that high. I finished hanging out my few items of clothing and went back to my apartment. I felt terrific.

From that day, anytime I ventured out into the garden and she was already there, she'd immediately stop whatever she was doing and walk briskly to her apartment building, head down, and mouth shut. I never spoke to her again.

*　　*　　*

After my run-in with the old woman, I noticed a distinct cooling of neighborly greetings from a couple of the residents, and one fellow in particular. Viennese are not generally overly friendly anyway, and I didn't consider it a great loss. This man was in his late thirties and had a wife and two small children, and I often met them in the hallway close to the main door of the apartment building.

He owned a very beautiful Rough Collie dog, and I would sometimes give it a quick pat as they went by. I like dogs, and dogs like me, and I am especially fond of shepherd dogs because I'm a shepherd, too. The Collie was large, about seventy pounds, and looked even larger because of its abundant blonde-and-white coat.

The second time I met them after the garden hose incident, I was coming into the apartment building and he, his wife and children, and the dog were coming out, although they were still inside the hallway passage, close to the main door. I greeted them and the man who was in the lead with the dog on a leash mumbled a cursory hello of some sort and then lifted the dog's leash and urged him forward to make what I assumed was a feigned attack on me.

I was very surprised and the dog, even more so. Collies are very gentle dogs for the most part, and he and I were friends. He moved only a small step and a half toward me and stopped. The man encouraged and commanded him again, but the dog did not obey.

"Mister, if you sic that dog on me, I will kill him right here in front of your wife and children. Is that what you want? That's a nice dog—much nicer than you deserve, you idiot!"

"I was only playing," he almost whined.

That's what all abusers say. I could see that he wanted to be shocked and disappointed, especially in front of his family, that the dirty foreigner did not appreciate his sense of humor.

He and the dog walked quickly and carefully around me toward the street, and his wife and children followed. If I am not mistaken, I think she gave me a quick smile as she passed by.

Needless to say, when it came time to vote for the "Friendliest Neighbor of the Year" award in my apartment complex, my name was not even on the list.

You can't win them all.

Public Transportation

I was once riding on a Viennese streetcar from my apartment near the Schoenbrunn Palace to the First District, downtown. Traveling by streetcar in Vienna is relatively slow, but it is always comfortable and always interesting. I like it. On that day, I was the only person in the car, except for the driver, but just in front of the main entrance to the Palace, a young lady climbed in the back of the car and proceeded all the way down the aisle to the front, where I was sitting just behind the driver.

She didn't say anything or even smile, and I really was not paying much attention to her until she sat down right next to me—close.

Well, I don't know about you, but in my experience that was an implied invitation that called for a response of some kind. I didn't know what to do. Should I put my arm around her? It was cold enough that day. Say hello? Talk about the weather? (You stupid country bumpkin!) I continued to stare out the opposite window and, like a complete fool, kept my hands folded in my lap. She said nothing and was leaving it all up to me, and I was not equal to the task. She had sat next to a boy when she had hoped for a man.

After three or four stops, she stood up and got off the streetcar at the West Train Station, and she crossed around in front of the car while we were stopped at a traffic signal. After she crossed the street, she turned around and looked at me, knowing that I would be watching from the window. She gave me a faint smile and walked away.

Jesus! She was ripe and available for, well, whatever, and I had done nothing. "Faint heart never won fair lady." And you know why I did nothing? I had not one, single, tiny mite of money, and it's hard to be cool and debonair when you're broke. I could not have invited her for even the smallest cup of coffee. Being a poor student in a fabulous city like Vienna can be very frustrating. But I will say this: It makes you tough. Going without eating, and sleeping in a cold room because you can't afford to heat it, gives you a focused determination that pampered folks just don't have. Read *Of Human Bondage*, by William Somerset Maugham. He writes about the value of money better than anybody I know.

On another day, in another city, and under more affluent circumstances, I was riding in the back of the 500 bus en route to Song Jeong Ri, a small town located just outside of Gwang Ju City. In the back of all city busses in Korea, there is a single seat for five passengers, which stretches all the way across the bus. I was sitting in the middle seat, and the other four were empty.

First, I would like to explain that whenever I happen to be riding on any bus or subway in Korea, the space next to me is always the last seat to be filled. It's not like Vienna. Most Koreans would rather stand up in the aisle than sit next to me. Hell, I don't blame them. I'm old and ugly, and for Koreans, I look just a little bit dangerous.

Anyway, I'm riding in the back of the bus and a young lady climbs in the front of the bus, and I could tell from the moment she ran her card over the automatic pay window that she was going to come to the back and sit by me. It was almost the same as my experience in Vienna, except the directions were reversed, and this time, I wasn't broke. There were plenty of empty chairs for her to choose from, but she disdained them all.

She pretty much kept her head down as she came to the back of the bus, but she looked up at me and smiled as she stepped up on the higher level, where the back-row chairs were placed. She sat down close to me and I spoke to her right way—not like that time in Vienna.

"I knew you were going to sit next to me," I said in English.

"I'm scared to death," she said. Koreans are generally very shy, especially with old, ugly, dangerous foreigners.

"Don't worry. You're going to be fine."

"I just wanted to sit by you and talk to you."

"I'm glad you did. Where are you going?"

"I'm going to Song Jeong Ri, to visit my boyfriend," she said.

"Well, he is a very lucky man to have such a beautiful and brave young woman like you."

"Really? He doesn't think so."

"You tell him I said so."

"Are you a teacher?" she asked.

"Yes, I'm passing through Song Jeong Ri on my way to Honam University. That's where I work and live. I like it out there in the country."

"Do you like Korea?"

"I do today."

She laughed and stood up to make her way to the exit in the middle of the bus.

"Goodbye," she said. "See you next time. Have a nice day!"

I waved as she got out. I love the 500 bus. It has always been my favorite.

Uncle Rudi's

My good friend, Fritz, had an uncle who lived in an old forester's house a few kilometers west of Retz and a couple of hundred meters south of the Czechoslovakian border. Uncle Rudi was a forest and gamekeeper for "the Countess," and he wore green loden, smoked a pipe, and carried an old rifle in his topless, old, green jeep. He was, perhaps, in his late fifties when I met him and was the genuine article.

Two or three times a year, Fritz and his Simmeringer friends and a couple of us foreigners would go visit Uncle Rudi, his wife, and their fair daughter, Gertrude, to spend a day, sometimes two, in the deep forests away from the big city, and we always had a wonderful time. At night, during the cold weather, we'd build a substantial bonfire to make music around and bake potatoes in the coals. Uncle Rudi, who was paper thin and about 5'8" tall, had a booming bass voice that could handle low C's with ease. His favorite tune was "Im Tiefen Keller," and in the appropriate accompaniment and perfect environment of the consumption of double liters of wine and generous amounts of beer, he would sing and all of us made music and merry until the wee hours of the morning. Those were great days.

One early autumn afternoon, about a week before all of us were to descend on Uncle Rudi and his ladies, Fritz and I met at John's to discuss how all of us would travel to Retz. Some would go by train and some by car. We did not have enough room in the two small cars, and we needed to plan the logistics of who went with whom, and how.

"Don't worry about me," I said. "I'm going to walk."

"What? You're kidding!" shouted Fritz. "You can't walk all that way."

"I'll bet you a case of beer I can."

"Done!" he said. "But wait a minute. You don't have enough money to buy a case of beer."

"I won't need it," I said. "I'll win the bet."

We shook on it with John as our witness, and we agreed that in every village or town I passed through, I would go to the post office and get an official stamp or signature from the local postmaster to prove I had, indeed, been there. It was eighty kilometers from the outskirts of Vienna to Retz, and there wasn't anything in between except a few small villages and hundreds of vineyards. I planned to walk through the country and sleep where night found me. My kind of trip.

If memory serves me right, I left on a Wednesday morning in order to be at Uncle Rudi's sometime on Saturday. The others were to arrive late Saturday afternoon, and that gave me three and a half days to make the journey. I had no idea how many kilometers I could walk in one day; it would depend on whom I met and what adventures might come my way. I was going to go with the flow and live off the fat of the land.

I took a Viennese street car over the Danube to Stockerau, the northernmost station in the city. There, I got out, put on my backpack, and started walking. Uncle Rudi's place was a few kilometers past the eighty kilometers to Retz, but I had almost four full days to complete the trip. No problem.

I don't remember many particulars of the first day of my journey except that I walked through the low hills of the Ernstbrunner Forest and saw practically no one. I followed two or three different roads that led generally north. They were not paved and changed from dirt to gravel, and then back again for no apparent reason, and sometimes were more path than road. It was very quiet and lonely, and I enjoyed holding my northerly course without benefit of a map or compass, although I must say it's pretty hard to get lost in Austria. There's a Gasthaus every three or four kilometers along the way and an occasional sign or two to keep you headed in a proper direction.

Late in the afternoon, I came upon a Gasthaus and stopped for a beer and ate a light meal. I had them wrap up a pair of sausages with some rolls and mustard with horseradish for my overnight camp, somewhere along my way, before I left the forest. I also took a couple of beers with me to wash down the sausages and to enable me to sleep more comfortably on the ground. The bottles of beer would be heavy, but I did not expect to walk much farther than a kilometer or two before I stopped for the night. Not long thereafter, I found a grassy spot off the side of the footpath and made my meager camp. The evening was going to be a bit cool, and I gathered some dry sticks for a fire before it got too dark to see. And it would be plenty dark. There would be no light to be seen anywhere, and I knew I was in for a splendid night for stargazing. I was tired from my first day's walk, and an hour after eating my supper and drinking the beers, I wrapped up in my ground cover, snuggled in close to the dying fire and, with my backpack as a pillow, lay down and went to sleep.

I awoke just before dawn and gathered my gear and stuffed it into the backpack. I took out the remaining sausage and roll and munched on it as I started down the gentle incline that would take me out of the forest and into the major wine-producing area in all of Austria and to the first village that had its name on the map, Enzersdorf im Thale. By my calculations, the small village was almost half the distance to Retz, and I planned to spend the second night there in a Gasthaus bed.

After the first thirty minutes, I easily walked out the stiffness of my first day's trek and the minor aches and pains that always result from a night spent on the ground, no matter how soft the grass, I deposited the empty beer bottles next to the entranceway to the first country tavern I passed by, although the place was closed and it would be a few hours before they opened. I knew they would not mind.

That morning, I put in some good kilometers and I waved to the friendly farmers as I marched by. Around 10:30, I stopped to visit with one farmer who was working in his vineyard close to the road. Since I had left the forest, the way had become a much more traveled farm to market road, and there were small farm tractors with trailers parked on the side and in the fields. He waved me over, and I leaned on his trailer while we talked.

"Where you going?"

"To Uncle Rudi's, up near Retz."

"Uh-huh."

"You own this farm?"

"Uh-huh, and my father owned it before me."

"Lived here all your life, I guess."

"Not yet," he said. "You in a hurry?"

"Oh, no. I've got plenty of time. I don't have to be in Retz until Saturday."

"Got time for a glass of wine?"

"I sure do," I declared.

"Follow me," he said as he led off up the hill through the rows of vines to a small door, which was placed in the side of a manmade cellar, underground, just below the natural crest of the hill.

He opened the door and preceded me inside. He left the door open to allow enough daylight to make our way about thirty meters down a roomy aisle with very large wooden wine barrels on both sides. We reached a break in the lines of barrels, and in the little underground clearing there was a small table with two straight-backed wooden chairs. It was an austere setting, at best, and above the table there was a single naked bulb, which hung down from a large wooden beam, which supported the earthen ceiling. There was a one-meter draw chain attached to the light switch, and the farmer reached up to pull the chain and turn on the light. Had it not been for the large and friendly wine barrels, the place would have been very grim indeed. There were two empty quarter-liter glasses placed on the table. Someone had known we were coming.

The man walked over to a small ladder and climbed up to the top of the nearest barrel and pulled out what I assumed was a large cork. He then picked up a long glass instrument, which had been lying out of view on top of the barrel. It had a long, hollow stem about a meter in length, and at the top, the glass ballooned out to about the size of a softball. The softball-sized section closed again and there was a one-and-a-half-inch lip, with a short neck, not unlike the mouthpiece of a trombone. From the top of the ladder, the farmer stuck the glass shaft into the barrel of wine and brought the mouthpiece close to his face. He exhaled, and then put his mouth over the lip and sucked the wine up into the glass balloon section. With his right hand, he covered the mouthpiece and then lifted the glass siphon out of the barrel and closed off the bottom section with his left. He told me to lift my wine glass up high, and he positioned the end of the stem just over my glass. He released his left hand and relaxed his right hand on top, and the wine flowed smoothly and sweetly into my glass. The whole process was a beautiful work of art, and I will never forget it. Of course, we then did the same for his glass.

He climbed down from the short ladder, and we sat in the two chairs and talked about I-don't-remember-what. The wine was excellent, and I thanked him for his country hospitality and made my way for the exit.

He came with me, and as we emerged into the bright sunshine, he asked me to wait a moment and he disappeared back inside the cellar. In less than a minute, he returned carrying a double-liter bottle of white wine. "Here," he said. "Take this with you in case you get thirsty on your journey."

I accepted with pleasure and put the large bottle in my backpack. There was plenty of room. Hell, there's always plenty of room for a bottle of wine.

It was now about an hour before noon, and I still had several kilometers to go before I reached Enzersdorf im Thale, although it would not be a lengthy march. I pushed on, enjoying my glass of wine, and hadn't gone over five hundred meters before I met another farmer who had seen me and my hat coming down the way and had walked over from his field to meet me on the road.

"Good day, how are you doing?"

"Fine," I answered.

"Where are you going?"

"To Uncle Rudi's, up near Retz."

"That's a long way to walk."

"No problem," I said. "I don't have to be there until Saturday."

"Good! Then you've got time for a glass of wine, right?"

"I sure do," I said, and he motioned me over to the trailer behind his tractor, and he took out a bottle from underneath a blanket and set up two glasses on the tailgate.

The bottle had already been opened, and he pulled out the cork and poured each of us a quarter liter.

We stood there and visited about the same topics that I continue to have forgotten from the first encounter, and we drank the white wine, which was equally delicious as the first. We drank rather quickly, and as there was a tiny bit left in the bottle, he poured us an even share of the remainder, and we drank that, too. I thanked him and said that I had to be moving on.

"Just a moment," he said, and again he reached under the blanket in the trailer and took out a two-liter bottle of white wine and gave it to me. "Just in case," he said.

I accepted the bottle but carried it in my hand as I got back up on the road. I would have been embarrassed to have him know that there was already a two-liter bottle in my backpack, and I was afraid I wouldn't be able to put it inside without the two bottles clanking together, thus giving me away.

I walked until I rounded a curve and was out of the second farmer's sight to sit down under a tree to rearrange my backpack. I took out my spare shirt and wrapped it around the second bottle before I slipped it in, next to the first one. I was satisfied that they would ride safely and silently as I pressed on. The weight of my backpack had increased substantially, and I had become a bit tipsy from the rather large amount of wine I had just consumed so quickly, on an almost empty stomach, and I began to realize that arriving in Retz by Saturday might not be such a leisurely deadline as I had earlier envisioned.

In keeping with those thoughts, I decided to take a short nap under the next available tree that would shade me from the noonday sun and to rest myself for the rigors of the afternoon's hike to Enzersdorf. No sooner said than done, and at the next shaded opportunity, I lay down on the increasingly comfortable ground, pulled my hat over my eyes, and went to sleep.

After about an hour, I awoke and continued on my way. The backpack seemed to have gained some weight while I was napping over the past hour, and my head was a little bit fuzzy from the morning's wine, but no matter, I would carry on.

I arrived in the village about thirty minutes before sundown. There was a single main street forming a T intersection with the second-largest and only other road to be seen—I must have been downtown. There was a Gasthaus at the middle of the intersection located on the smaller road, and I went in, shucked off my backpack, and sat down. There were several of the local guys around, but they didn't pay me much heed, which suited me just fine. I ordered a beer from the owner (at least she acted like the owner and was the only woman in the place) and drank half without putting it down. It tasted wonderful. Now, that wine is the devil's drink, especially before noon, but that's another story.

I asked the woman if she had rooms for the night. She said she had no rooms to let, but a lady at the end of the street had extra rooms at her house. She pointed down the street on the road I had not come in on.

"It's about fifty meters from here. You can't miss it."

And she was right.

"Do you want something to eat?"

"Later," I said. "I'll go get a room and come back."

At the end of that street, there was a large, imposing, three-story house, which created a cul-de-sac. It was an old house with a porous, unkempt fence, which provided a warning to any motorist who might come that way to stay out of the yard. There were chickens and rabbits running free around the house, and there was a large, gray guard goose, which stood at the gate, blocking my way to the main door. For those of you who may not know, a goose protecting the property is a force to be reckoned with, and I don't mean maybe.

I stepped up to the garden gate and the goose stood tall, almost five or six feet on the other side of the fence. I opened the gate and stepped inside. The goose wagged his tail and gave me an open-mouthed hiss and stood his ground. His head was six inches higher than my belt buckle and was weaving back and forth like a cobra. I had brought no stick with me and left my tennis racquet at home and, quite frankly, didn't know what to do.

At that moment, I heard a shout from the street behind me, and a dirt clod sailed over my shoulder and struck the goose full on the chest. He backed off and I jumped for the front door. From the safety of the small porch, I looked back and gave a thank-you salute to one of the lads who'd come after me from the Gasthaus. He was laughing and walked past without saying anything.

There was an old knocker on the door, and I lifted it and slammed it up and down at a polite volume three or four times and waited. Nothing. I kept a close eye on the goose, but he had given up somehow, and evidently as long as I stayed on the porch, I was okay. I knocked again with my knuckles with the same result. "Is anybody home?" I called out; it was a big house and maybe she couldn't hear me. I knew somebody had to be at home. Country people never go anywhere. Who'd feed the chickens and the rabbits and the goose? I waited around for a few minutes, ever mindful of the goose, but I was not going to have any luck. I went back to the Gasthaus and told the boss-lady that nobody was home.

She laughed. "Oh, she's in there, all right. Wait just a moment and I'll go with you," she said as she disappeared back into the kitchen.

I waited and she returned quickly, and we walked back to the house together.

When we got just outside the gate, she shouted, "Hanni, open up! There's someone here who needs a room for the night."

Immediately, a very small wooden door, about a foot and a half square, opened high up on the third floor just under the gable, and an old lady's head stuck out the empty space.

"Whattaya want?" she shouted back.

"This gentleman wants to rent a room for the night," my benefactress shouted again.

"How do I know he won't kill me?" the old woman shouted.

"For God's sake, Hanni, he's a very nice young man. He won't hurt you and besides, you need the money."

(I didn't tell her I'd been drunk as a skunk before noon that day.)

"Hrummph!" the old woman snorted and pulled her head back inside the house.

She came down, shooed the goose away from the gate, and agreed to let me have a room. I thanked the boss-lady and told her I'd be back to her place to eat supper as soon as I washed up. The old lady showed me to my room, and I paid her on the spot. That helped her disposition.

Supper at the Gasthaus went without a hitch, schnitzel with a green salad and French fries, and I gave the owner one of the double liters of wine as a tip for her very excellent service to a stranger passing through. I asked her to keep the tip a secret, because I would not want either of the farmers to know I had taken their generosity in such a cavalier manner. It was a very small, tight community, and there were surely no secrets, especially concerning a foreigner walking through the countryside. She swore to secrecy, an oath I took with a large grain of salt. In addition, she was kind enough to sign, stamp, and date my travel document so that I could prove to Fritz that I had made it this far.

That night at the old woman's house was one of the most unpleasant I've ever spent. It was a very small room with a single bed that was adequate, but unfortunately, the blanket she gave me reached only from my shoulders to about four inches above my ankles, and the hordes of mosquitoes in that room seemed to have not eaten for months. I guess they were mosquitoes; I was afraid to look down there. They acted like alligators.

I left at daylight and she saw me to the door. She'd probably been up for hours, barricaded in her room with a loaded shotgun across her lap. I declined a cup of coffee and slipped out the front door with all senses on red alert for the gray goose. The goose was not in evidence, thank God, and I went through the garden, walked down to the only intersection in the village, turned left between a couple of houses, and headed north, to Retz.

The scenery between Enzersdorf im Thale and Retz is charming, with gentle sloping hills, which are perfect for vineyards, and several small forests interspersed throughout. The hills are rather large and several hundred feet above the flat lands, but the lengthy, gradual inclines of the paths and farm roads make climbing the hills very pleasant. When one reaches the top, it's always a pleasurable surprise to enjoy the panoramic view from such a high outlook and realize that the climb's gentle grade made the efforts involved hardly noticeable.

On the last two days of my journey, I stopped in three or four very small wine villages to get official confirmations from the most important person I could locate, and they gladly signed my paper and added stamps and seals to signify that I had passed through. It was great fun, and several of the kind folks told me that they wished they could accompany me. Of course, I invited one and all, but there were no takers. On both days, I was offered more wine than ten people could have drunk, and I did accept enough to be polite and neighborly, but I had to cover the distance and too much wine would not have been helpful. In addition, my feet were beginning to hurt and by late on the third day, I could feel blisters popping up in all the usual places. I was getting smarter, though, and throughout that day I turned down all bottles of wine offered to me to take along for the trip.

At one point on Friday afternoon, a farmer drove by me on his tractor pulling an empty trailer. He came to a stop as he pulled even and asked if I wanted a ride. Now, Fritz had bet me that I couldn't walk all the way to Retz. That was the deal. If I were to ride, that would be cheating. Did I want a ride? Hell, yes, I wanted a ride! I looked around to see if there were any spies lurking about, and of course there was no one to rat on me, so I put my backpack in the trailer and climbed in. It was wonderful. He drove up the hill for about one hundred fifty meters and—I promise I'm not making this up—drove off the road and into a field and stopped.

"Okay," he called back at me. "This is it. End of the line."

That was it? I had to start walking again? Hell, not even Fritz would have called that cheating. I got out of the back of the trailer and kept on going.

I slept in a field that Friday night, and the ground was so soft and I was so tired that my blistered feet did not bother me so much. It didn't hurt that sometime during the afternoon I had made up my mind to sacrifice the double-liter bottle of wine that I had been lugging around for a day and a half. I figured out that carrying the wine in my stomach was much easier than carrying it in my backpack. Smart boy. I had picked up some small rolls, sausage, and cheese at the last village I visited, and when I stopped for the night I slowly ate the sandwiches I put together and continued to do my best with the wine. The large bottle was intimidating. Had the wine been in two one-liter bottles, I could have done much better, but as it was, I drank about half before I gave up and went to sleep.

At daylight the next morning, I was already on my way. I had put on my last clean pair of thick socks and then pulled the tired, old dirty socks over them to give my blistered feet a bit more cushion. It worked pretty well, and I knew I could last out the few remaining hours of my journey. The half-empty jug of wine I left under the first tree I came to on the side of the road. I'm still slightly embarrassed about that, because I did not want to litter the pristine countryside, but I also did not want to carry it anymore and this was Austria's Wine District, for God's sake, and anyone who found it would understand and know what to do with the remainder.

It's comforting to be up early and watch the sun rise. For one thing, it helps you figure out what direction you need to be taking. For those of you who aren't quite sure, if you want to be going north, like me, that sun should be on your right when it comes up. I figured I needed to head a few degrees to the west of due north to arrive in Retz, and if the sun was true (and it always is), I was spot on.

I made good time that morning and arrived in another picturesque village around noon. It had a wonderful fountain in the town square, and I quenched my thirst at an attached trough that had probably been used by livestock, the town folk, and wandering pilgrims for centuries. The water was sweeter than the wine, and a lot lighter. As I was wiping my mouth on my sleeve, Texas country style, one of the locals walked up and asked me the usual.

"To Uncle Rudi's, just west of Retz," I replied.

"Ah, I know him well," he said. "The forester?"

"That's right. How much farther is it? I'd like to be there by mid-afternoon."

"It's not far at all," he said. "Come with me and I'll show you the way."

I followed him to the small white church, about forty meters distant, and we went inside and before I started to get suspicious, he opened a small door in the anteroom and began climbing the clean, narrow winding stairs to the belfry.

"Leave your backpack there on the floor," he instructed as he went up.

The bell tower rose handsomely above the church roof, about thirty feet above the ground, and at the top, there was space for us to stand and survey the countryside. It was a bright day; the air was crystal clear and it was all just about perfect. I couldn't have bought a better day. He pointed in my intended direction.

"Look, that's Retz right there." (Retz has only four thousand inhabitants but is a substantial town by Wine District standards.) "By this road here," he pointed to the street we were on, "it's two and a half kilometers to the city hall on the main square. But Rudi lives one and a half kilometers to the west, up in those hills over there. You don't need to go into town. Rudi's road comes in just south of town, and you'll need to turn left at the edge of town. There's a Gasthaus called 'The Bear,' and you'll need to turn left there. You can't miss it."

And he was right.

When we descended the stairs, I asked him if he would sign my paper, which I was using to record my journey. He did so with pleasure and wrote two short sentences to Uncle Rudi as well. I thanked him for the very charming and helpful interlude and set out for "The Bear." I arrived in less than an hour and went inside to have a beer and rest my aching feet. The guys inside took more interest in me than the others I had encountered over the past three and a half days and asked me several questions about where I was from, why I was walking, and how much farther I expected to go, seeing as how the Czechoslovakian border was only a very short distance away.

"Oh, I'm just going to Uncle Rudi's," I answered. "The forester."

Of course, they all knew him, and one of the fellows said he was driving up that way and would be glad to give me a ride. I hesitated, but what the hell. I'd already cheated once, and one more time wasn't going to hurt. Besides, the road to Uncle Rudi's was seriously uphill and my feet needed some relief.

"I accept with pleasure," I said, and drained the rest of my beer and picked up my backpack.

We went outside and he pointed to a tractor and trailer exactly like the mode of my last eight-wheel transportation.

"Climb in!" he shouted cheerfully as he mounted the tractor and cranked her up.

This time, I made it all the way to Uncle Rudi's house, and my chauffeur knew exactly where to stop and drop me off. I hopped out the back and waved and shouted my thanks as he drove away. I had done it. Enough to win the bet? Well. We'd just have to wait and see.

The forester's house was located in a small partial clearing of an acre or so and was set about thirty meters off the road. It had a single story and a deep cellar, as befitted Uncle Rudi's favorite song. The outside walls were a dark gold color; perhaps at one time they'd been that bright Maria Theresian yellow of the palace at Schoenbrunn, but the weather and surrounding forest had stained and mildewed them to a much darker hue. The roof, porch, and trim were painted in a dark Loden green, which blended in perfectly with the imposing and, in the late afternoon and evening, ominous presence of the encroaching forest. In the clearing, there were several trees close to the house, and even on the brightest days, only the noontime sun provided direct light and warmth that reached the ground unfiltered by the natural leaves and branches.

The two ladies had heard the tractor halt and came out of the house. Gertrude ran to the edge of the yard and gave me a huge hug and kiss. She had a fabulous slim body, but she was strong as an ox. Her mom was a bit more reserved but glad to see me all the same. Gertrude took my backpack and led me to one of the comfortable chairs, which were in the front garden, and I sat down and loosened my boot strings. I took off my boots and peeled off the two pairs of two- and three-day-old socks and gave my blistered feet some much-deserved and much-needed fresh air. When the ladies saw the condition of my feet, they rushed to get a small washtub, soap, and some cool water, which Gertrude placed the tub on the ground before me. I stuck my feet in the cool water, and as she washed and bathed my feet, I thought I'd died and gone to heaven. Then Mom brought me a beer and a hearty homemade plum schnapps, and my welcome to the dark forests of Austria, on the edge of the Czechoslovakian border, was complete.

The others arrived around mid-afternoon, and the Simmeringer Boys and the other foreigners all brought wives and girlfriends and boyfriends and several compatible combinations thereof. It was a jolly crew, and we were in for a great weekend.

Uncle Rudi bravely came home in the late afternoon and greeted everyone warmly, with a shy grin and a handshake all around. He was a taciturn man, and I don't think I ever heard him utter a sentence of more than five or six words. But when he did speak, we all shut up and listened. He was that kind of a man.

Everyone except me had brought magnificent things to eat and drink, and Uncle Rudi and his ladies did not have to put themselves out unduly to feed the rowdy group. That morning, they had managed to cook up a huge amount of potatoes from their garden, which provided an excellent side dish for just about anything the visitors might have brought. That night, we built a large bonfire behind the house and baked potatoes in the hot coals and sang a thousand songs accompanied by guitars, recorders and large amounts of beer and wine. I do remember that I left my potato, which was wrapped in foil, in the hot coals too long, and when I retrieved it from the fire it floated like a balloon. It was light as a feather, and when I opened the foil, the peel was still intact, but the insides had vanished completely.

On Sunday morning, most of us had recovered enough to start milling around by mid-morning. Some folks slept in the house, but most wrapped up in blankets and sleeping bags and slept outside. Somebody had planned to send out a party to gather schwammerln (mushrooms) from the forest, and we went out in the jeep and on foot to harvest what the early autumn forest still had to offer. We brought back a lot and the ladies cleaned them and dipped them in whipped scrambled egg batter followed by a coat of flour on each side, and then they fried them in deep cast iron skillets like southern style chicken-fried steak. Most of the mushrooms were white, relatively flat, four or five inches in diameter and three-quarters of an inch thick. We ate them with some of the leftover potatoes from the night before with a hot, brown sauce that was made from scratch that morning. Delicious!

In the afternoon, Uncle Rudi brought out his beautiful, breech-loading single shot .22 rifle and we tacked up a couple of targets on a large tree next to the barn, to find out who was the best shot. Now, with a .22 rifle, I am about the best I ever came across, if I do say so myself (or I used to be before I started wearing glasses). I won the shoot-out, but barely. Gertrude placed a very close second, because she was used to the gun and was a fine shot in any case. She was somewhat miffed that I beat her. If I had been just a little bit smarter, I would have shot high and to the right on the last shot, placed a gentlemanly second, and possibly reaped the rewards that a first-place finish, at least in that contest, simply did not have to offer. But hard-headed, Texas cowboy pride got in my way and I went back to Vienna with a hollow victory to complement my hollow head.

The case of beer? Fritz and I declared our bet a draw, and a couple of weeks later we both chipped in and bought a case for the Simmeringer Boys which we all consumed with our customary delight.

The travel document I had taken with me to get signatures, stamps and seals from responsible officials to record my short journey through the Wine District, I gave to Fritz. It was interesting and unique, and he was pleased to accept it, and I suspect he still has it somewhere, snug and safe, locked up, way down "Im Tiefen Keller."

Walter and Julia

L ate one summer morning, I was in my apartment on Simmeringer-hauptstrasse, and the phone rang. It was my good friend, Walter. He had a magnificent bass voice.

"Hey, Jackie!" he said. "Let's go swimming."

"Okay, when do you want to leave?"

"I'll pick you up in an hour. Be outside on the street."

"Fine, but can I bring my girlfriend, Rosa, along? She's visiting me for a few days. She's from Spain."

"Jackie, only if she's good-looking."

"She's very good-looking," I assured him.

"Fine, I'll be there in an hour."

Walter and I were studying at the Musikhochschule and were classmates in the opera school. Rosa and I had been friends for about a year. I met her in Heidelberg when I had sung a bit part with the Heidelberg Opera. She was from the Pyrenees Mountains in Catalonia and taught German to Spanish and French guest workers in Heidelberg. I had stayed with her about six weeks in that city, and she was very influential in helping me learn German as well. She was perhaps five feet tall and weighed about ninety pounds in the rain. Her diminutive size notwithstanding, she was an excellent representative of those wild and passionate folk from that mountainous region and was a lot of fun and tough as a boot. She backed up for nobody.

We packed a small bag and were waiting for Walter and his wife, Julia, at the appointed time and place. They picked us up and we drove to the Danube River Canal, which is a favorite Viennese swimming location with several beaches to choose from. We pulled up in a large parking lot, which already contained several cars. The area was not downtown, but one could see many high-rise buildings and there was a large rustic park with hotdog stands and small riverside huts for weekend residents.

Before we got out, Julia said brightly, "Okay, everybody, take off your clothes."

I looked at Rosa to make sure I had heard her correctly. My ability with the language was still a bit shaky, and taking one's clothes off too soon, at the wrong place or time, can have embarrassing consequences.

"Did I hear that right?"

She had a big grin on her face and she nodded yes. I climbed out of the back seat and observed Walter and Julia undressing, and with a valiant effort at nonchalance and savoir faire and some other French stuff, I took my clothes off, too. Rosa had already stripped naked and was helping Walter take the cooler and barbeque equipment out of the trunk. I grabbed hold of the cooler and at the last second, Walter threw me a volleyball from the back of the car. He slammed the trunk shut, and we left the parking lot and marched, single file, on a path through a pasture over a small rise and descended to a tree-lined swimming and camping area.

On the way, I shouted at Walter's back, "Hey, Walter! What are we going to do with this volleyball? The cooler I understand. Come to think of it, I could have a stiff drink right now, if we've got time to stop. We're not really going to play volleyball, are we?"

"Sure, Jackie. We always play volleyball."

"In the nude?" I asked incredulously. The thought of playing coed volleyball in the nude with a bunch of people, maybe ten on a side, strained, yea staggered the limits of my imagination. But it was probably more suitable than leapfrog, I guess.

"Don't worry," he said. "It's water volleyball."

"How deep's the water?"

"Waist deep," he replied.

"I'm ready. Let's go."

We arrived at our barbeque area, which had a couple of picnic tables and a large covered shed with a concrete floor and no walls. There was room for about fifteen or twenty people. As is customary in Austria, everyone shook hands with everyone else and self-introductions were made all around. One young lady in our party got up off her outdoor chaise longue and swayed over to me to introduce herself and shake my hand. She had the most fabulous breasts I have ever encountered or even imagined, and as she approached me they floated delicately, yet generously, like whipped cream on hot chocolate in a gentle breeze. I looked her straight in the eye and hoped my hand met hers. She gave me a firm grip and declared she was pleased to meet me. I assured her I was extremely pleased to meet her, too.

"Anybody for volleyball?" I called out. (Not really, I was cool and didn't gawk. Even Rosa said so.)

"Come let me introduce you to my grandparents," she said.

You bet! I could hardly wait.

Rosa and I followed her to another table, and she motioned for an elderly couple to join us. The gentleman got up and limped away from the table. He had only one arm, and his body was riddled with bullet wounds. Heck, this was just like Beirut. I was beginning to feel better already.

After a short visit with Oma and Opa, we unpacked all our things and enjoyed the warm summer afternoon, and for about an hour, everything was pretty much normal.

The nude barbeque was rather ordinary, except for having to keep a sharp lookout for the flying sparks. I helped with getting the fire started and the beer drunk. After a while, several of us trooped down to one of the manmade lakes next to the river and we did, indeed, play volleyball. Rosa had some difficulties playing, because waist deep for most folks was neck deep for her, but she wasn't interested in volleyball anyway and she splashed around and had a good time. After an hour or so, we were called back to the barbeque area to eat sausage and chicken, and a great time was had by all.

For me it was all surreal. Here we were, standing out in the middle of this pasture eating barbeque and drinking beer, and not one person had on any clothes. What if Quanah Parker and fifteen screaming Comanche bucks mounted on wild mustangs had come hellin' over the crest of the hill to rip our party to shreds? We would be helpless. All we had to protect ourselves were a couple of volleyballs and some plastic forks, and I was forty miles from my loaded pistol. Just thinking about that made me nervous, and I immediately ate another piece of chicken.

Finally—and I mean, at last—the party broke up, and in the fading sunlight of the late afternoon, we packed our gear and returned through the pasture to the safety and comfort of the car. We loaded our gear, and I have never been so happy in all my life as when I put my pants back on. I laughed at Rosa as I cinched up my belt.

"Happy now?" she asked.

"Damned right! How 'bout you?"

"I had a great time."

I knew it didn't matter to her whether she had on any clothes or not. She probably hadn't even noticed.

On another day, and perhaps another year, I dropped by unexpectedly at Walter and Julia's house and rang the doorbell.

"Just a moment," I heard her voice.

Then the door opened and there stood Julia, as naked as a jaybird, holding what looked to be a kitchen towel in her hand.

"Jackie, how nice of you to drop by," she said. "Please come in."

She stood aside and I walked in.

"Come into the kitchen, if you don't mind. I'm in the middle of a big project. Sit down and I'll pour you some coffee."

The kitchen was large and in the middle, there was a breakfast table with four chairs. I sat down and she remained standing at the counter doing whatever I had interrupted.

"I hope you don't mind that I'm without clothes on."

"No problem at all," I assured her. "Be comfortable."

Julia was tall, blonde, and slim, and as far as I was concerned, she didn't have to put any clothes on for the rest of her life.

We chatted while she worked, and the coffee did justice to Vienna's reputation as having some of the finest coffee houses in the western world, although the service at Julia's had to be the best. After about fifteen minutes, she sat down across from me at the table and we continued to visit.

Shortly thereafter, the apartment door banged open, and Walter come in with a big smile.

"Jackie, how are you doing?"

"Terrific!" I said. "I'm enjoying your wife's very wonderful hospitality."

"Julia!" he declared with a grim face. "Have you no respect for your husband? Get up and get me some coffee, too."

He sat down and laughed and winked at me as she obeyed.

"She lets me be the boss sometimes."

We all knew that Julia was the boss—all of the time.

Walter was kind enough to leave his clothes on, and I was grateful for that.

We all moved to the living room, and I don't remember how long I stayed. But I do remember that not one word was mentioned about Julia's being completely naked the whole time I was there. Cool!

Customs at Christmas, Beirut, 1980

During Christmas of 1980, I travelled from Cedar Falls, Iowa, to Beirut to spend the holidays with my wife's family in that city. My wife and baby daughter had already left in late November in order to trade the Iowa winter for the sunny and comparatively warm days on the eastern coast of the Mediterranean Sea—not a bad idea. The "situation" at that time was rather calm, and I looked forward to spending a couple of weeks in that exciting and exotic city.

My wife had called me and asked that I bring some things for the baby that were hard, or impossible, to find in the war-torn area, and I, the world's lightest traveler, carried two large suitcases with me when I boarded the plane in Des Moines.

It is a long way from Iowa to Lebanon, and I don't remember anything of particular interest about the flight, but it must have taken at least thirty hours. I arrived in Beirut in the mid-afternoon, and from the airplane window, as we made our approach to the airport, which is located in the southern portion of the city, there was no battle smoke rising from anywhere, as far as I could tell. It looked peaceful and very beautiful.

When I disembarked, I could hear no small arms fire, and except for a large number of heavily armed Lebanese army soldiers who were scattered all over the area, the airport was not much different from the airports in Des Moines or New York City—except it was, of course. Fighting could break out at anytime in Beirut, especially at the airport, and it was often engulfed in serious fighting for its possession and control.

I went inside, picked up my bags, and stood in the short line waiting to go through customs. It would not take a long, because Beirut was not one of the favorite Christmas destinations in those days.

I stepped up to a low counter and put my two suitcases on top. The soldier who was to check my bags was about six feet tall, slim, and very handsome, with jet-black hair, olive skin, a small moustache, and a well-trimmed beard, which lined his jaw. He was carrying an AK-47, which had seen plenty of use and was very comfortable on his arm. He was in his mid-twenties and had been around.

"Open your bags, please," he said in perfect English.

I opened the first bag to reveal my usual stuff, which would interest nobody. I still travel that way. Basic stuff. Used jeans, socks and underwear, a couple of corduroy shirts, and a sweater. I checked to see if he wanted to rummage through it all, but he wasn't interested. He motioned to the other suitcase.

"What's in the other bag?"

I looked him straight in the eye and said, "Two hundred fifty baby diapers and a stuffed alligator."

I watched him closely as I spoke, and the tiniest upward curves at both ends of his mouth gave him away.

"Welcome to Lebanon," he said as he motioned me through.

Service Taxis: Beirut, 1983

My first unaccompanied trip from the apartment to my new job at the university was very interesting and enlightening. Actually, my wife gave me a ride to the university that morning and she told me to take a service on my return. On the way to work, we drove through Ashrafieh to the sea, turned left, and took the port road to the West Side. We passed through a couple of causal checkpoints near the Green Line, but the crossover was uneventful. Near the American Embassy, we turned south and drove up the hill to the university main gate, a distance of about a kilometer. She dropped me off and returned to our apartment in East Beirut. Before she drove off, she cautioned me one more time.

"They're (the service cars) the ones with the red license plates. Don't get in any car unless it has a red license plate!"

"I got it," I said.

The service was a private taxi that went to a specific location on a specific route. As long as you wanted to go in his direction, you could ride as far as you wanted for the equivalent of 25 cents US—a very good deal. Nevertheless, anybody could flag down the service at any point along the way and climb in for the same price. I met some very interesting people and had some very interesting experiences during the ten months I spent in Beirut. On two occasions, the service was stopped and fellow passengers were dragged out of the car and shot on the sidewalk. I once delivered a baby in the back seat, but those are stories for another day.

Throughout my first day on campus, I had a great time meeting my new students and faculty colleagues, but I waited until late that morning to ask one of my Lebanese colleagues about taking a service in order to get home.

"Where do I catch a service?" I asked one of the younger fellows.

"I have no idea," he declared rather strongly.

"I saw a lot of them on the streets as I came to school. Surely there's a stop close by."

"I've never taken a service in my life! I really don't know anything about it," he said as he walked quickly away from me.

In my next class, I asked the students where I could get a service to take me home. They all laughed and told me that not one of them had ever ridden in a service.

"It's too dangerous," one said, and they all agreed.

"We take a regular taxi or hire a car," they explained.

I found out further that most of them had drivers on call when they wanted to go somewhere. My students were all very well-to-do, and I was just a poor country boy with no chauffeur. For the next couple of hours, I asked several people about the service, and nobody on that campus had ever taken a service—at least the ones I spoke to hadn't. I was beginning to be a little nervous, because I had talked to three or four guys who looked pretty tough and got no positive response.

On the bright side, I visited with Malouf, an older Lebanese faculty member, and he was able to tell me that when I did finally track down a service, I should tell them I wanted to go to the Mathof. I had no idea what that meant, but I practiced it about a hundred times so that I could get it right, if and when the time came.

At around 3:30 that afternoon, it was time for me to leave the campus and head for home. I wasn't overly concerned, because I knew I could walk home if necessary. It was five or six miles and I knew the proper direction. In addition, at that time there was no street fighting going on, and if I were careful and crossed the Green Line at a proper place, walking across the city would not be a problem.

As I came out of my theater office, a young man was waiting for me in the hall.

"Professor Jack, follow me and I'll show you where the service stand is. It's very close to the campus."

I went with him out the main gate and walked straight about thirty yards down the hill.

"It's right here," he said as we came to the first intersection. "Just wait here on the corner and one will come by every two or three minutes. You won't have to wait long."

I thanked him and waited until the first old Mercedes with a red license plate showed up. I signaled him to stop and I leaned in the window on the passenger side. "Mathof," I said with a confidence I did not feel.

He raised his eyebrows slightly and drove off. Raising one's eyebrows in Beirut means no.

A couple more cars drove up, with the same results. The driver of the fourth car, after some slight hesitation, motioned me to get in and I climbed in the back. I passed him the 25 cents and I was on my way.

We drove to a very large five-street intersection in Barbir that was jam packed with street vendors and buyers of all sorts of shapes and descriptions. It was a crazy, busy place. It was impossible to drive through the intersection, so drivers just stopped at the edge, turned around, and went back in the opposite direction.

The driver stopped and motioned for me to get out, and I asked, "Mathof?" and he pointed in a northeasterly direction and said something that I, of course, did not understand.

I started walking through the market area in the direction he pointed and took what looked to be the most probable street. I left the intersection area and, after about seventy-five meters, came to the Muslim Checkpoint, which was the last stop before crossing the eight hundred meters of the Green Line, the no-man's land between East and West Beirut. As I have mentioned earlier, there had been no fighting in the city for two or three weeks, and the guards waved me through without checking any ID or asking any questions.

The road to the opposite side was straight, passing on the west side of the Hippodrome, and I passed thirty or forty people coming the other way. People were very friendly and seemed to be very relaxed. There were no cars passing through, only pedestrians. Author's Note: There were no bicycles, either. Nobody rode a bicycle. I never bothered to ask why, but I assumed that a person on a bicycle, moving along at a moderate clip, was a target that was irresistible for the young cowboy sharpshooters. I think the same can be said for the complete absence of birds in Beirut. I never saw one bird in Beirut during my sojourn there from August 1983 to June 1984. Not one. Birds aren't stupid. They got the hell out of there.

Passing through the Christian, East Checkpoint was as easy as the Muslim side. I didn't even slow down as I went through. There were several taxi drivers lined up just on the other side, and I took the one at the head of the line.

"Sin-El-Fil," I said with increasing confidence and made a circular motion with my hand to indicate the traffic circle, which was very close to my apartment.

My place was only about a mile from the checkpoint, and we arrived in very short order. The taxi cost about two dollars at the most. Not 25 cents, like the service, but still a bargain.

After a few days of traveling back and forth, I realized that the service cars and taxis did not travel from one side of the city to another. On each side, the drivers would take you to the Green Line, and you would get out to walk across to the other side and get a new car and driver. The Mathof (the National Museum) was on the East Side, and that's why the drivers were hesitant to pick me up on that first day. They knew I didn't know what I was doing or where, and how, I was going.

Almost all the service cars were old model Mercedes-Benz's, and I got to know many of the drivers quite well in my daily travels. They were all very friendly and helpful, many spoke German, and not once did I ever have a problem with any service drivers during my stay in Beirut, although I thought one driver tried to cheat me one time. I got in the service to ride shotgun up front and gave the driver the 25-cent fare. He shook his head and indicated he wanted more money.

"I know the price," I said. "It's 25 cents, and I'm not going to pay more."

There were two young ladies in the back seat, and they said, "Oh, no, it's okay. Today the price is 50 cents."

"And why is that?"

"Today is a dangerous day, and all the drivers charge double when it's particularly dangerous to be out on the streets."

"That's fair enough," I said, and forked over the additional 25 cents.

Get yourself blown to a thousand bits for only four bits. Hell, it's still a bargain. Keep the change.

I eventually became the resident expert at Beirut University College in traveling back and forth across the city. All the faculty and staff lived on campus or in West Beirut, and the students whose families lived in East Beirut seldom visited their parents there. When they did go across, they often asked to go with me and I always obliged. I knew the territory.

Taking the service was a major part of my daily life in Beirut, and I cannot imagine having missed it. I learned the people, the common folks, like me, and the pulse of life on the street in that fabulous, exciting, cosmopolitan, and dangerous city.

Beirut Professionals

I met with two or three students on the sidewalk in front of Gulbenkian Theater the other day. We were talking about music and one of the fellows, who was not in any of my classes, asked me why I didn't offer a recital for the students on campus, saying that it would be a nice thing to do. He was right, of course, but I do not enjoy giving recitals, although I love the song repertoire and I know about six hundred songs. Opera is better suited for my voice, personality, and ability. I did not explain all that to him but simply said, "I'm a professional singer and I only sing for money."

And with a perfectly straight face, he replied, "I understand. I'm a professional killer and I only kill for money. But you're my friend and I'd kill you for free. Come on. How about giving us a concert?"

I didn't know if he meant it or not, or if it was just an example of Beiruti black humor. I chuckled as best I could and said I'd consider it.

Later on that semester, my wife and I did give a joint recital and it was quite successful, if I say so myself. My wife was an excellent singer, and I sang well enough to keep up with the company.

Before our recital, we were interviewed by a newspaper reporter. I was to sing several of the "Old American Songs" arranged by Aaron Copland, and she was concerned that my last number was "Zion's Walls," a dynamic, foot-stomping revivalist tune of the nineteenth century.

"You're going to sing this piece about the praises of Zion, by a Jewish composer, here in this city?"

"Yeah," I said. "I never thought about it."

"It might get you killed."

Well, I went ahead and sang it anyway, and nobody took a shot at me, at least not at that time. We sang a couple of Gershwin tunes as well. It's hard to put together a musical event of any kind of western art music without having Jews involved in one way or another. It's especially tricky in Beirut.

Practical German

Many of the service taxi and regular taxi drivers in Beirut spoke German. It was a strange phenomenon, and I finally asked one of the drivers to explain it to me.

"We all go to Germany to work for two years and save enough money to buy a good, used Mercedes. Then we drive it back to Lebanon and become taxi drivers. Of course, we learn German while we are there."

Almost all taxis in the city were Mercedes-Benz's, and I cannot imagine how the city could survive without them. At that time, the late 60s and 70s models were the workhorses and are probably still going today.

The service taxis had red license plates. For twenty-five cents (fifty cents on dangerous days), you could flag one down and climb in if you were going in the direction the driver was headed, or the direction of the first paying customer. Anybody could signal the driver and get in. It made for strange traveling companions from time to time. Very strange.

I once got in the front seat of a service and there was a uniformed militiaman in the back seat. I did not pay any particular attention to him, but the driver, whom I knew, immediately started speaking to me in German.

"You're from Vienna, right?" He was very direct.

"That's right," I said. "Actually from Simmering, the Eleventh District."

"I thought so," he said.

The guy in the back seat said in English, with a loud voice, "Hey! Do you speak English? Aren't you American?"

He was looking for trouble. I looked back over my left shoulder, but not enough to be polite.

"I speak English okay, but I'm from Austria. Vienna."

"I thought you were American," he slurred. He acted drunk, although people were seldom drunk on Beirut streets.

"Sorry," I said, and I smiled as I looked back at him.

He was dirty and thin and had a scraggly-assed beard, and with his right hand he was tossing a hand grenade up and down in between the seats. He was missing a couple of front teeth and grinned at me in a goofy and slightly dangerous sort of way. I guess he was waiting to see what I would do or say. I didn't react at all and turned back to face the front and directed the driver to let me out about five blocks before my normal destination in Bourj Hammoud. He pulled over casually, and equally casually, I got out and closed the door. He drove off before the idiot in back could get into any mischief, and he might have saved my life.

Anyway, I appreciated his good offices and his judicious use of German and hoped that the cretin sitting behind did not pull the pin on that grenade. Come to think of it, by getting rid of me, maybe the driver saved his own life as well, but I didn't think about that until later.

Hamburgers and Picasso

Around 3:00 one Thursday afternoon, I locked up my office and climbed the stairs to the ground floor of Gulbenkian Theater and walked out the glass front doors. There were five or six students waiting for me to accompany them across the Green Line to East Beirut, the Christian side of the city. This was an unusual occurrence, because I almost always went alone. I crossed the Green Line daily, but the university's students lived on campus or close by and were not accustomed to the uncertainties and sometimes very dangerous situations that were quite common when traversing the city. They wanted to go with me, the shepherd from Texas. Not that there was much I could do for them, one way or another; it was all I could do to take care of myself, but I was a veteran in making my way over to the other side, and I guess I made them comfortable.

We traveled in two small private cars, which probably belonged to friends of the students, and drove quickly to the drop off spot in Barbir, a large market area and intersection located about one hundred fifty yards southwest of the Muslim Checkpoint on the Green Line. We climbed out of the cars and walked across the market and up to the checkpoint. It was not crowded, and I was a bit nervous because we were close to 4:00 and that was normally my cut-off time to cross. The cowboys, located on both sides and in taller buildings along the straight crossover road that went past the Hippodrome and onward to the National Museum, were always starting to get restless with the approaching evening and sometimes became trigger-happy around 4:00. I always maintained that the cowboys had to take their early afternoon naps and woke up grumpy along about mid-afternoon. In any case, the later one crossed over, the more dangerous it became.

We walked through the checkpoint without being stopped, and I nodded to a couple of the guards I knew. We saw each other almost every day, and they knew who I was. Besides, that afternoon, they were busy drinking coffee. That afternoon we walked the entire distance, approximately eight hundred yards, without incident, and as it was a lovely spring day. It was like a walk in the park—a walk in the park with electricity in the air that kept one ready at any time for instant action. I walked across the Green Line some three hundred times the year I was there, and it was never boring. We chatted while we walked, and one of the young men, who was not known to me, asked me how long it had been since I'd had a hamburger.

"About eight months. Seems like eight years," I replied.

"My father has a restaurant and he makes great hamburgers. Why don't you join me this evening and we'll have a very nice time. All the others (our crossing companions) are coming, too."

"Wonderful," I said. "Where and what time?"

"We'll meet in Bourj Hammoud at 8:00. Do you know Bourj Hammoud?"

I said I knew.

"Do you know that white Volkswagen van that is always parked in the first large intersection just east, off the main road to Jounieh?" Somehow I got the idea that he already knew I knew about the van.

"Yes, I do," I said. "I always buy my Armenian beer and Irish whiskey from the fellows in that van. It's a good place to shop."

"Good. See you there at 8:00. If the van's not around, just wait at the intersection and we'll find you. My father's restaurant is about a minute and a half from there."

I bought it. In those days you had to be careful in Beirut, but this kid was on the up and up. In addition, one of the girls in our party was my student, and she would have told me or made a signal of some sort if this guy were not to be trusted. Besides, Bourj Hammoud was predominately Armenian, and therefore my territory. I had family there, and it was just about the safest place in Beirut, certainly for me.

After the crossing, we parted company and I went to my apartment in Sin-El-Fil, showered, and put on clean clothes. The apartment was deserted, and I assumed everyone had gone to the mountain house to prepare for the long weekend, which began on the morrow. I relaxed on the veranda and watched the traffic from my fourth-floor vantage point. It was a very interesting highway and passed ten feet in front of the door to my apartment. It was the road to Damascus, and it was extremely busy until around midnight, every night. Heavy trucks, festooned with hundreds of colorful doodads, gewgaws, and gadgets of all shapes and descriptions, slammed through gears in both directions as they navigated the dangerous journey between the capital cities. I always kept an eye out for Paul, who must have taken this very same route when he met the Big Man while "on the road to Damascus." Funny, but I always felt his presence there. It was a very ancient way.

At 7:30, I left the house and grabbed a service to Bourj Hammoud. He let me off very close to my point of rendezvous, and I walked the short distance to the intersection. The white van was in its usual position, parked with several other vehicles in the middle of the large intersection, and I waited on the sidewalk, which was elevated about a yard off the road surface and, therefore, much safer. Traffic in Beirut must be seen to be believed, and I'll comment on that at another time.

My new friend appeared at the appointed time and guided me through a couple of very narrow passageways to his father's restaurant. Two or three times, the buildings were so close together that I could touch both sides at the same time. We arrived at a small open courtyard, about thirty feet square, and sat down at one of the two or three tables. There was a single tree in the middle of the yard, I guess to offer shade from the noonday sun. The buildings surrounding the yard were four or five stories high, and the sun would shine inside the area only at high noon, and perhaps thirty minutes before and after. It was comfortable and secluded.

"Where are the others?" I asked.

"They'll be coming soon," he said, and indeed, they showed up almost immediately.

We made room for the others and ordered hamburgers, beer, and arak. We visited for about ten minutes and the young man, who had been away from our table, appeared with our waiter and said that his father would like to meet me, and would I be so kind as to follow him to his father's office inside. I was immediately suspicious and realized that this hamburger evening was a setup of some kind—and probably had been all along.

I got up slowly and followed him to the courtyard entrance of the restaurant, where a thick, burly man awaited us. He was about 5'10" tall and weighed close to two hundred twenty pounds. There was no fat on him, and he moved with deceptive grace when he opened the door and motioned me inside, ahead of him. I politely declined and motioned him in ahead of me, and he smiled and went through the door first. I followed along behind him and the owner's son followed me. It was a dark, narrow hallway, and we had to proceed in single file. We came to a door after about thirty feet, and the big guy knocked softly and walked in. I followed him inside, and we entered a small office with a desk and sofa that looked and felt normal in every way, except there were no windows. It looked exactly like a restaurant office to me. A handsome man got up from behind the desk, stretched out his right hand after his son introduced us, and said he was pleased to meet me. He spoke in Armenian.

"Please sit down," he continued and motioned me to a rather small chair next to the sofa.

The son excused himself and said he was going back to join our party in the courtyard. I objected, saying that I had used up all my Armenian vocabulary and that I was afraid my hamburger might get cold.

"Don't worry," he laughed. "My father speaks excellent English and would like to speak to you in private for five or ten minutes, not more. After that, he'll treat you to all the hot hamburgers you can eat!"

I agreed and remained seated. The big guy left also, and the father and I were alone.

"Would you like a cigar, Professor?" he asked in English.

"No thanks, perhaps after dinner."

"Of course."

We chatted for two or three minutes about life in Beirut and "the Situation." There was never any difficulty in finding a topic for small talk in Beirut. Interesting things happened by the minute.

Then he asked me. "Do you know anything about painting?"

"Well, I've painted several houses in my life, and I must say I'm pretty good at it. The scraping's the hard part. I have done inside work, too." His office could have used a fresh, new coat.

"That's not the kind of painting I meant," he said.

"What kind of painting do you mean?" I asked.

"Artwork. Very fine paintings. Masterpieces, perhaps."

"Well, Mr. Avakian, I've been to a couple of museums and I have seen a few famous paintings, but I'm a musician. I teach music and a bit of drama and acting. I know next to nothing about fine painting. But Virginia, my colleague, knows a great deal about art. I'm sure she'd be glad to assist you."

"I doubt it," he said. "I have a painting I'd like you to take a look it, if you would be so kind," and he reached into his top desk drawer and pulled out a photograph.

He handed it across the desk to me, and I took a look. I was surprised, to say the least. It was a Picasso from the Blue Period, painted just before 1910, I believe, and was of a man and woman standing on the beach with a small child. Famous as hell.

"You have this painting?" I asked.

He nodded.

"Here?" I asked, looking around the little office.

"Oh, no," he laughed. "In a safe place."

At that time, there was no such thing as a safe place in Beirut. Everything was protected by the business end of an AK-47 or an MI6, depending on which side of the city you were on, and if you were outnumbered or outgunned, none of your so-called possessions was safe.

"You have the original painting? Here in Beirut? This painting is worth millions of dollars. Somebody will slit your throat for this painting. Heck, I might even do it myself!" I can't believe I said that last sentence, but he didn't take offense.

"Oh, I don't think so," he replied. "You see, that's why I asked my son to bring you here this evening."

I waited.

"You see, we know about you here in Bourj Hammoud. We know what you did for us in Istanbul, and we are very grateful. You can be trusted."

I said nothing.

"I know you are planning a trip to Vienna in two weeks. If you will take the painting with you to Europe, I will give you half of the selling price."

"That would be a lot of money," I said. "But I wouldn't know to sell such a thing, even if I were able to get it out of Beirut, which I highly doubt. How would I carry it? Under my arm? Somebody would slit my throat for your painting. No thanks."

"If you could get the painting to Vienna, I have contacts in Brussels and they would come and take the painting off your hands. You wouldn't have to sell the painting yourself, just transport it to Vienna."

I didn't bother to ask him how he, a hamburger restaurant owner, happened to be in possession of a priceless work of art. That would have been indelicate. But his possession of the painting was not out of the realm of possibility, especially in Beirut. You could buy anything off the streets—crystal chandeliers, grand pianos, fine china, precious stones—and you didn't even have to get out of your car. You could do it from your open car window and if you could agree on a price, they'd load it in your car for you. You'd have to dust whatever it was off a bit, but Lebanese streets are dusty and that was part of the deal, and one of the reasons it was all so cheap. Another reason was, it was all stolen—100% profit, not counting a few murders here and there.

A few weeks earlier, I was window shopping along the street, about two minutes' walk from the hamburger joint, and a man appeared from nowhere and asked me if I'd like to step inside the shop, because he had something to show me. I had been looking at some binoculars in the window display, and I agreed. It was a sporting goods store, interesting to me, and he was friendly. It was a small shop, and he asked me to wait just a moment and he disappeared into the back. He returned in less than a minute with a long, beautiful box in his hands, which he placed on the glass counter and opened it to reveal two elegant side-by-side shotguns.

"They're handmade from Spain," he said. He took one out and handed it to me. "They are matched, and perfect in every way."

I broke the gun to make sure it wasn't loaded, eased it shut, and put it to my shoulder to track a mourning dove coming in over the stock tank at fifty miles an hour, dodging and weaving, and gently squeezed the trigger. Bam! I missed again. No matter. They were works of art, .410 bore, and smooth as silk. I knew a lot more about shotguns than I did about Picasso. Unfortunately, I had no use for such beautiful guns in Lebanon. For one thing, there were no birds. I never saw a bird in Lebanon. Perhaps there were some outside the city, but in Beirut, not one. All the ones who could still fly had left the country long before I arrived. The only game to hunt in Lebanon was people, and a .410 was a little bit light. But I wanted the guns.

"How much?" I asked.

"Three hundred dollars for both," he said with a completely straight face.

They were worth at least 3,000 dollars, maybe more. It was a steal. Literally.

"I would love to buy the guns," I said, "but I don't need them here in Beirut and I'm sure I could not get them out of the country" (proven later to have been absolutely correct).

"I understand. But they are very beautiful, are they not?"

"Yes, they are," I agreed.

I asked to see some good binoculars, which I bought for sixty bucks. Like the shotguns, they were worth at least ten times that amount, and when the time came, they were very helpful in getting me out of the country. They have been my faithful companions for almost thirty years, and at this moment, they are two yards from my left elbow, and I will keep them until the day I die.

Meanwhile, back at the hamburger restaurant, I returned to my table in the courtyard and joined my student friends. Mr. Avakian was as good as his son's word, and our money was not good for that entire evening. He was also kind enough to bring me a fine Havana cigar, the availability of which was one of the pleasures of living in Beirut. All things considered, it was a very interesting and pleasant evening.

The Picasso? I later checked, and if my memory serves me right, the original is hanging in the National Gallery of Art, in Washington, D.C.

Maybe.

Escape to the East

In February of that year (1984), the Amal Militia took over the west side of the city. Whether or not they controlled the whole Muslim area, I don't know. Somehow I doubt it, but at least they controlled the area with which I was familiar.

When the fighting started, I was on campus and there I remained for almost a week within the relatively save confines of the walled university campus. Of course, had any group of fighters wanted to come on campus, they could have done so at anytime. The student clubs, which maintained a guard at the two large gates to the campus, would not have offered much resistance even though they were armed with AK-47s, and even if they were disposed to do so. Nevertheless, the campus was free from the vicious street fighting that surrounded us, and it was probably the safest place to be in West Beirut.

The first day, there was substantial heavy weaponry in action. The campus was hit by a few rockets and there was heavy .50 caliber machinegun fire, with mortars and tanks dueling in the streets throughout West Beirut. That afternoon, several of us went up to Gordon's beautiful, large apartment and drank the afternoon away while listening to music on the inside and heavy percussion on the outside. We did complain to Gordon that his apartment was located on the third floor, on top of the outside southern wall of the campus, and that the windows, which provided such a magnificent view on normal days, also provided clear shooting for any sniper who might want to harm us, or any passing shell that might accidentally come our way. We didn't complain too loudly, however, while we were partaking of his very fine liquid hospitality.

Late that afternoon, I went down to my office, two floors underneath the Gulbenkian Theater, to do some work and check on my classroom. My assistant, Marcel, was in my office at my desk and listening to opera on our stereo. He got out of my chair and sat down on another chair, and I sat in my customary place.

"You doing okay?" he asked.

"Sure. A bunch of us have been over at Gordon's having a pretty good time, I must say. But it sounds a little rough outside."

He shrugged. "I'll call my father tomorrow and ask him what we should do. Today's too early, but if it keeps up, I'll give him a call late tomorrow afternoon."

Marcel's father was a retired colonel in Interpol and was a very heavy hitter in certain circles, including the streets of Beirut, which were the circles where we would be needing some assistance.

"Where are you going to spend the night?" he asked.

"I guess I'll sleep up on the stage. Just wrap up in one of those curtains on the stage left side. There's plenty of them there and it should be comfortable enough. Also, it's a good place because it's below ground level. Be hard for a rocket or artillery shell to reach there. A good place, I think."

"Well, I might join you," he said.

"No problem. There's room enough and curtains enough for several people."

The fighting in the streets seemed to escalate in the late afternoon and early evening, and Marcel and I stayed in my tiny office and listened to music and discussed opera and singing. He was an aspiring opera singer, and that's all he talked about. I could not interest him in learning to read music, however, and despite my efforts, he always told me he could hire a pianist to teach him the music. He was right, of course, because he had tons of money. Everybody at Beirut University College had tons of money, except for me and the other faculty members. The students were rich.

I left the office and went over to Joe's for a short visit and a quick sandwich, and then I returned outside to the courtyard area to sit under the trees on one of my favorite benches. I didn't stay long because there was no one else stupid enough to be outside, and because the trees would offer scant protection if a rocket were to come my way. I went back to my office and cleaned up the choir room, which was the classroom for all my subjects. The room also had a very fine Kawai grand piano, but I did not feel like practicing.

Along around 10:00 P.M., I went back to the apartment building where Gordon lived but did not return to his place. It was too wide open and was on the top floor in his section of the building, and that was the worst place to be in any fighting situation. In small and heavy artillery barrages, the top floor is almost always hit first and suffers the most damage. Stay off the top floor.

I walked down the main corridor of the ground floor, away from the cafeteria, and ran into five or six faculty members who were camped out on the landing and first two or three steps of one of the stairways leading to the apartments on the upper floors. It was as safe a place as any, and there were no windows in the corridor at that particular spot. That part of the building was made of substantial limestone rock that would deter all but the heaviest and most prolonged bombardment. It wasn't as safe as my underground office, but the women were a lot better looking.

"Hi, Jack. Sit down and join us," they chimed. "We're having a party!"

"Don't mind if I do," I said and took a proffered beer and sat down on the floor.

It was quite dark, as the electricity was not functioning, but we could see well enough. They were a jolly crew in spite of the receiving and sending of tank and artillery fire in the neighborhood, and we joked and had a good time (at least I did) for over an hour. Except for Virginia, all were Lebanese teachers who lived close to the university but were afraid to take a chance on going home. For whatever reason, they did not want to ask to spend the night in a colleague's apartment, so they would be making a night of it right there.

Just before midnight, I took my leave, telling them I was going to the theater and wrapping up in one of the curtains and sleeping on the stage floor. It was not going to be comfortable, but I have slept in worse places. I walked down the hall to the east exit and slipped out the door. The path to the theater was a circuitous one that wandered about forty yards through a stand of pines, over a small bridge, and up a short flight of stairs, which rose to an outdoor concrete walkway, which was attached to the outside walls of the theater building.

I was halfway around the curve of the building, still outside, when I realized someone was following me. There was a shadowy figure moving quickly and quietly through the trees on the same path I had just come, thirty seconds before. There were no lights, but I could see well enough because my eyes had become adjusted to the darkness over the past two hours. For some fortuitous reason, there was a small niche in the theater wall that presented a perfect hiding place for me to await my silent pursuer. I stepped inside the vacant space and waited. I heard light steps on the walkway and realized it was a woman who was not overly concerned with being discovered. I stepped out of my hiding place so she could see me when she was still about fifteen feet distant. I did not want to scare her unduly, or follow along behind her if she were to pass by without noticing that I was waiting for her. It's scary out there. She stopped abruptly when she saw me and I could hear her quick, very audible intake of breath, but nothing more.

"You are following me," I said.

She didn't move or answer.

"Why?"

"I am going with you," she said.

"Come," I said, and led the way inside the building, through the patron doors of the main theater, down the graded aisle on the stage left side, and up onto the stage itself.

Earlier, I had shaken out and folded two of the curtains for my own use, and I spread them both out on the floor and motioned for her to sit down. She did not, but remained sanding. I had planned to sleep on one and cover up with the other, but with my unexpected guest, I folded them twice and put both on the floor to sleep on. I then took another curtain from just off the stage and took it out into the seating area and shook the hell out of it to knock off the major chunks of dust and dirt. She did not seem to care if the curtain was not just super clean, and I returned to the stage, took off my jacket, and roiled it up to make a pillow for her. She finally sat down on the pallet and moved the jacket over to my side and patted it, indicating it was for me to use. I lay down on my back and brought up the curtain to cover us. She lay down close to me and put her head on my upper left arm and shoulder and snuggled up tight, with the top of her head right underneath my chin. She then put her left arm around my chest and didn't move until daylight. There was fighting in the streets throughout the night, but as far as I could tell, she slept like a baby.

I had left the main doors to the theater open, and at around 6:00 A.M., a small amount of light filtered down to the stage floor. Without a word, she sat up, put her shoes on, and walked out.

Over the next three or four months, I passed her on campus several times and she would give me the tiniest nod of recognition and would almost smile. We never spoke and she never acknowledged that she even knew me at all, or that I even existed, really. I respected her obvious desire not to be associated with me in any way, and after that, when we did meet, I was never more than professionally polite to her.

As soon as the cafeteria opened that morning, I went for a cup of coffee and some sweet bread. The battle sounds of the street fighting had died away, and it was a beautiful morning to sit out on my bench under the trees and enjoy the temporary quiet and the fresh air. I brought a coffee with me from the cafeteria and planned to nurse it along for an hour or so. The fighting cowboys were all sleeping late, and I figured we would have some relative peace and quiet until early afternoon.

When I left the cafeteria, I had stopped at the South Gate and observed that the streets were deserted. It was also very quiet on campus, and nobody was out and about until Joe came out of his apartment and joined me on the bench.

"Good morning!" he said as he approached. "Sleep well last night?" He had a beautiful bass-baritone speaking voice, was an excellent actor, and was a crappy singer. He was an English Ph.D. from somewhere important and was a distinguished teacher. (Joe later became President of the American University in Leysin, Switzerland.)

"I slept fine, considering the circumstances. Have you seen Marcel? He was supposed to join me on the stage last night, but he didn't show up. Maybe he got a better deal."

"That wouldn't have been difficult. I wish you'd have come over and slept with us. It's got to be more comfortable than the stage floor."

"It is, of course. It's also a hell of a lot more dangerous at your place." Joe's apartment was along the north wall of the campus, but on the second floor. It wasn't as dangerous as Gordon's, but it had windows opening out onto the street. Risky. "It's much safer on the stage, below the ground level."

"Well, you're right," he agreed, "but there's no Russian vodka in the freezer, is there?"

"You know I don't have a refrigerator, much less a freezer. I've got a cooler, though. But no ice."

"Why don't you come over for lunch and we'll have a short drink before noon. The fighting will start up again at about that time, and we want to be ready."

"I'll be there," I said.

"By the way," he continued, "Silva called and said that she and the children have gone up to the mountain house and for you not to worry. Just take care of yourself and come home when it's safe."

I was not able to call them at the mountain house, but there was no need for me to worry. East Beirut was quite safe and the mountain house even more so. All I had to do was take care of myself and be patient. The heavy fighting would not last forever. Classes would begin on the morrow (Monday), and I would work with those students already on campus and any of the hearty ones willing to take the chance and come to school—and there world be some. Several of the dormitory students came out on campus, and we visited and had a good time. Until the fighting started again, it was almost like being on vacation 'til noon.

After a nice lunch at Joe and Teny's, he and I wandered over to Gordon's for round two of whiskey and Willie Nelson—an excellent combination, I might add. I was not overly familiar with Willie's music, and the days I spent at Gordon's were of some professional benefit. Most of what we did at Gordon's was bullshit, but not all. The most important thing I accomplished that day was to wash my clothes. I had an extra pair of pants and a shirt I kept in my office for just such emergencies as this, but everything needed washing. Gordon was kind enough to wash it all and provide me with the bottom half of a karate outfit to wear around the house while my laundry was being done.

We whiled away the afternoon, listening to sporadic small arms fire in the neighborhood, and doing I-don't-remember-what, and after my clothes had dried enough, I put on one ensemble and took the other clothes to my small office and hung them up to dry. I met Marcel on the way, and he informed me that he had spoken with his father and that he had told us to wait, and that when the time was right, he would send a car for us. "We should do as he says," Marcel said. "My father never worries about me and never tells me what to do, but if he tells us to wait, then that's what we should do."

Fine by me. I had clean clothes, albeit somewhat wet, and had drunk enough to be in an excellent mood. I could wait forever. The rest of the afternoon passed pleasantly enough, and the evening, too. That night, I slept again on the stage floor, but by myself this time.

Monday morning I was up early and went for coffee at the cafeteria. I met Gordon there and he looked a bit rough around the edges.

"Man, if I just hadn't had those last eight drinks last night!" He was a very funny guy. "You going to teach today?"

"I'm going to try," I said. "I have only one class this morning, at 10:00. I guess some students will show up. We'll listen to Beethoven and I'll help them with their term papers. If only a few show up, I can give them individual attention with their writing. You going to your office?"

"Yeah, I'll go over and wrestle with the Ice Princess." Gordon was second in command at the library, and his boss was a Lebanese woman. Aida somebody, in her early thirties, extremely beautiful, and cold as a splitting wedge. He had it tough. He got up from the table and said, "Well, I'll see you later. I've got to go patch the fresh bullet holes in my office walls."

"Okay, see ya."

I finished my coffee and walked outside to return slowly to my office. As I went passed the South Gate, I heard my name, "Jack!, Jack!" and one of our students was running toward me, looking very upset—almost crying. "Can you help me?" She was short and cute and wearing a bright red dress.

"I will if I can. What's the problem?"

"They're going to steal my car!" she cried. "I want to bring it inside on campus, but the guards won't let me. Only faculty members can drive a car on campus."

"Where is your car?" I asked.

"It's right outside on the street. Please hurry, because they're stealing the cars right now. I have a new car and I don't want to lose it. Please, please bring it inside!"

She took me by the hand and pulled me to the open gate, and I looked to the right, up the street. I didn't like what I saw. The street went straight for about sixty yards and then curved to the left, out of sight. On both sides of the street were walls, the university south wall, which was fifteen or twenty feet high, and a lower wall on the other side. There were no driveways or intersections, just the walls. From around the corner, and at least halfway down toward the university entrance gate, six or seven black-hooded young men, armed with AK-47s, were moving quickly down the street taking all the cars that were parked on both sides. I was very impressed with the business-like way two of the guys would swing under the cars and, in a matter of seconds, get them started and the doors opened to be driven away by one of their cohorts. The two who were slipping under the cars so professionally were rather thin, perhaps one hundred forty-five pounds, and moved underneath with such simple grace that they could have been dancers. Maybe they were. Dancing thieves.

"Which one is yours?" I asked.

"That little red one, right there."

She pointed to a small, brand-new Fiat, which was parked on the university side of the street, almost equally distant from me and the militiamen. There were three or four cars in front of hers and about the same number behind. If I started walking immediately, at a normal pace, I would arrive at her little red car before the thieves, but not by much.

"Here are the keys," she said. "Please hurry!"

Well, quite frankly, I didn't want to go. Those cowboys had probably been shooting at other cowboys for the last three days solid and were probably not in the mood to be trifled with. I think it was the black hoods that bothered me. Tough guys with guns have never impressed me very much, and I've run into a few, here and there. They do not frighten me. Nevertheless, this time, I was afraid. The combination of the black hoods with the eye slits and their lithe, professional actions made me very nervous. But I had to do it. Hell, I'm from Texas. Several students were watching to see what I would do, and the armed guards at the gate, also university students, were keeping a close eye on it all. They would not interfere, one way or another, and I did not ask them to.

And so, I started walking calmly, keeping my hands in the open so they could see that I was not armed and didn't have a hand grenade stuck up my sleeve. As I approached the car, I showed them the car's keys, with a bright pink plastic ornament, for God's sake, and the militiamen watched me closely but did not make any significant move to stop me. The two fellows starting the cars just kept on working and moving in my direction. I unlocked the car door, got inside, moved the seat back, and cranked the engine. I pulled away from the curb and drove the car slowly the twenty yards to the gate and turned inside. Made it! Not sure why. Maybe they had already stolen enough cars that day. Maybe they had already killed enough people that day. Maybe they appreciated my efforts on behalf of a Lebanese student. Maybe they liked her pink keychain. I don't know why, but it worked. The young lady thanked me profusely, and a couple of the guys clapped me on the back and that was it. Another day, another dollar in Beirut.

It was not long before my 10:00 class would begin, so I walked back to my office to prepare just one more time. I had been doing practically nothing for the past three days other than sitting in my office and dodging bullets, and I was more than prepared for my Music Literature class. Only four of five students showed up, and I helped each of them individually with their papers and their writing. They all wrote quite well, considering English was their third, fourth, and sometimes fifth language. They enjoyed the unexpected one-on-one attention, and so did I. After class, I went to the cafeteria for lunch and ran into Gordon again.

"Is your bar going to be open later this afternoon?" I asked. I knew he had to be at the library until at least 5:00.

"Not today, it's not," he declared.

I was surprised. "You sick and tired of all of us coming over to your place?"

"Hell yes, I am! But that's not the main problem. You ungrateful bastards have drunk up all the hooch, except one bottle of the Irish, which I've hidden from you vultures, so at least I'll be able to have a drink after I'm alone, and without any booze. I'll probably be alone most of the evening!"

I almost felt sorry for him, but it was a very serious problem indeed, and I told him I would check around and see what I could do.

"Well, you're going to have to do something this afternoon, if possible. I can't help because I'll be locked up with the Ice Princess all afternoon. God, it makes me thirsty right now just thinking about spending the whole afternoon with her!"

"Aw, man. Give her a little bussi (Austrian dialect for a short kiss) and pat her on the butt. She'll love it."

"Bullshit! Get outta here!"

I laughed in a sympathetic sort of way as I left and told him not to worry. I went to Joe's to draw up a plan of action.

"This is grim news," he said after I related my conversation with Gordon.

"The problem is," I said, "since the new militia has taken over, I'm not so sure what their policy is on drinking alcohol. They're supposed to be pretty damned strict about demon rum, and the rumor is that they're going to segregate the beaches, you know, the women on one day and the men on the next. Shit, we might have to just go swimming—a draconian idea. Anyway, we'd better be damned careful."

"You know any of the guys at the South Gate? Are any of them your students?"

"I don't think any of them are my students, but I got acquainted with some of them this morning. We get along fine."

"There's that big grocery store down the hill on the left, just across the first intersection. They've got plenty of supplies if we wanted to chance a trip down there, and back, of course."

"I'll go," I said, "'if you go take up a collection from the regulars. I'll check the temperature of the guards at the gate."

"Good. Let's meet outside at the tennis courts in half an hour."

I left his apartment and went across the courtyard, about fifty yards, and walked over to the guards.

"Good afternoon," I said.

"Good afternoon," they replied with big smiles. They were the same guys who were manning the gate earlier.

I came straight to the point. "Now, gentlemen, we've got a problem here on campus. We have drunk all the whiskey, arak, and beer, and there's not a drop left." (I didn't tell them about Gordon's one, last bottle.) "I want to know if it's okay with you if some of us go down to that grocery store on the corner and bring a large supply of alcohol."

"Sure, no problem. That's fine," they said.

"It's okay? I want to make sure there is no misunderstanding."

"It's okay. It's fine," they repeated in a very cordial manner.

"Is it safe?" I asked.

"It's safe," they assured me.

That was easier than I thought. Too easy? I didn't think so. They were on the level.

I went back to wait for Joe and sat down on one of the benches. About fifteen minutes later, he appeared with Alaan and Jesse in tow. (Alaan Steen and Jesse Turner were later kidnapped by the Hezbollah organization and held captive for four years. Jesse had the most enlightened idea about how to solve the fighting in Beirut in particular and in all the Middle East in general. "Put silencers on all the guns," he said. It's the best solution I've ever heard, before or since.) All three had backpacks, and Jesse was pulling a stout-looking wagon. He was a big guy with a large beard and looked funny pulling a child's wagon.

"What's the verdict?" Joe asked.

"We've got the green light. Didn't seem to be any problem at all."

"Well, let's get started," he said, and we all marched over to the gate and the fellows waved us through.

We turned left on the street, and before we had gone ten feet, we were joined by two young men on motorcycles, each armed with an AK-47, to make sure we got the goods bought and brought to the house in just the way we wanted.

They next day, I met two morning classes and we listened to music and quit early to go outside and enjoy the campus and fine weather before the fighting would start again 'round noon. The fun of it all was beginning to wear off, and I wanted to see my wife and children and get the hell out of West Beirut. The campus was becoming rather small.

There was a rumor floating around that all westerners who could make it to the U.S. Embassy on Wednesday would be given a helicopter ride from the Embassy to an American ship located about ten miles out to sea and would then be taken to Cypress and be flown out of the Middle East. It became fact later in the day, and I was determined to make my way to the Embassy early the next morning and see if I might be able to hitch a ride to Jounieh, about fifteen miles north of Beirut, and then catch a ride, or hitchhike, or walk back to the other side of the city and get out of this mess. I knew that a new U.S. Embassy office had just been opened in Jounieh, and I thought there might be a possibility of getting there. I did not want to go to Cypress. I just wanted to go home to my family.

That Tuesday afternoon and evening passed slowly and somewhat tediously, in spite of the fresh supply of alcohol that we all had presented to Gordon as soon as he returned from the library. We deposited ninety percent of what we had purchased at his place, and he had to quit bitching about all us freeloaders. I continued sleeping on the stage floor, but it was becoming very uncomfortable and I was excited to be leaving the campus early Wednesday morning to make my way down to the Embassy. All who could make it to the Embassy by 9:00 A.M. would be offered a helicopter ride out of Beirut, to freedom and normalcy. There was a catch, though—getting there. I had spoken to Marcel of my plans the night before, and he rose early to see me off.

"If you don't make it," he said, "can I have the stereo and all your books and recordings?"

"Of course, but don't starting carting everything off just yet. Besides, I'm not going to leave the country. I just want to get to the other side of the city."

"I am aware of that," he persisted. "I mean if you don't make it, period."

"And I am aware of that," I said. "The answer remains the same. Yes. Do you want it in writing?"

"No, that's okay. Nobody but me wants it anyway." (The silver-tongued devil)

"Just give me a few days," I said.

"Don't worry," he said, "I will," and he kissed me three times on my cheeks, Lebanese style.

The trek down to the American Embassy was about a kilometer and, normally, a very pleasant walk. It was located on the Corniche Mazraa, a beautiful avenue that ran along the shore of the sea on a seawall about twenty or thirty feet above the water. It was a fabulous location. My way from the university would take me almost due north with a drop in elevation of about two hundred feet. The way led through the Hamrah area, which contained many restaurants and beautiful shops. Hamrah was very cosmopolitan, fast-paced, exciting, and often dangerous as hell. There were more dangerous places, but they were located farther south, closer to the airport, and to the Shouf Mountains. I had been to Hamrah many times, and I knew the area well.

I left the campus through the North Gate and walked straight down the street for two short blocks, and then I turned right and walked through a residential area, parallel to the main street below, for another two blocks. It was becoming clear that I was to be the only person on the streets; it was very eerie and completely deserted, except for me. Normally, the place was hopping with activity even at that early hour. All the folk obviously knew something I didn't, which was nothing unusual, but it was a beautiful day and people should have been up and about. Everything glowed with wonderful, early morning sunshine. There was an exhilarating, brisk wind, and the air was crystal clear. However, in spite of the wind, it was deathly quiet and as I turned left to head toward the sea. I could hear and feel the solid drone of a B-flat pedal point emanating from the sixteen-foot pipes. Despite the visual beauty of the day, underneath, it was spooky and, it seemed to me, deadly. I continued my journey trying to took and feel as happy as I could, but that walk to the Embassy was one of the strangest experiences of my life. I crossed Hamrah's main street and marched cheerfully, yet carefully, all the way to Corniche Mazraa without seeing a single soul. The T intersection was about two hundred yards east of the Embassy, so I turned west to reach my destination. Finally, I could see a few people in front of the Embassy building and there were two helicopters, one on the ground and one at a very low altitude approaching the landing area. With the ships in the harbor, the bustling helicopters, the wind-whipped waves smashing powerfully against the seawall, and the fabulous Mediterranean sunshine, it was a splendid scene.

The Embassy staff had put a large desk out in the middle of the front lawn, and there were some official-looking men in evidence. As usual, as befitted any gathering in Beirut in those days, there were tough-looking guards who were armed to the teeth. There was one who always wore a baseball cap, and I had met him around town (on the West Side) on several occasions. We nodded in recognition. The past fall, my wife and I had given a recital on campus and the American Ambassador had been in attendance. The dude in the baseball cap had stood in the middle aisle of the bottom floor throughout a major portion of the music making. At the recital, he wore a very expensive blue blazer and gray trousers, sans baseball cap. He was a blue-eyed blond, handsome, very dangerous, and was obviously a man appropriate for all events and venues.

Perhaps the most impressionable thing at the Embassy (for me, that is) was the wonderful green grass of the front lawn, and I believe it was the only grass I had ever seen in Beirut. It was one of my main complaints about the city and the small portion of Lebanon that I knew, that there was no grass anywhere for the children to play on—just red, sandy dirt. Now, I like red, sandy dirt just fine, but there ought to be a little green grass scattered around here and there. Just my opinion, of course.

I walked up on the lawn and asked to speak to someone about leaving the city. A man motioned for me to sit in one of the straight-backed chairs that were lined up, horizontally, about twenty feet in front of the desk, and he informed me that a clerk would be arriving soon to arrange for my passage. I sat down and relaxed and enjoyed the view. Looking around, I was somewhat concerned that the small group of people out there on the lawn was extremely exposed, and there was no place to hide or take cover if some of those mean cowboys might want to take a few shots at us. It's a useful little habit one picks up after being in a city like Beirut for a while. You've always got your eye out for the closest place to hunker down. You don't want to be indecisive if the bullets start flying; you need to have a place already picked out, just in case.

It seems as if I waited forty-five minutes or so before the clerk showed up. In the meantime, a few more people had arrived, including a man with his wife and two young children. I don't know how far they had traveled to get to the Embassy, but with a wife and two small children, it must not have been easy. When the clerk finally sat down and set up shop, I told the man with the family to go first. All I had to take care of was myself. He had his hands full with family and all the bags they could carry. He accepted and was very grateful.

"Thank you very much," he said. "I really appreciate your generosity and good manners."

"No problem. I'm probably not going anywhere anyway," I said, but he was gathering his small flock and had ceased to listen.

After they had signed up and moved toward the helicopter pad down the street on the East Side of the Embassy, I stepped up to the desk.

"Good morning," we exchanged greetings.

"Where is your luggage?" he asked.

"Right here," I said as I pulled my toothbrush from my right-front jeans pocket.

"That's it?"

"That's it."

"You travel light!" he smiled.

"Damned right, I do!" I declared, "especially in this town. But I have a question. I don't really want to go to Cypress. I would like to fly, or go by boat to Jounieh if someone is going there today. My family is on the other side of the city and I just want to go home, not leave the country."

"I'll see what I can do. I'm not sure if anyone is going to Jounieh today or tomorrow, but I will check and see. Please be patient and I'll find out for you as soon as I can. It shouldn't take too long."

I sat back down and waited while he checked seven or eight more passengers to Cypress. The helicopters were not large, and it didn't take long to fill one up.

After another thirty minutes, he got up and came over to me and said, "I'm so sorry, but there is no plan to go to Jounieh. You can leave for Cypress in a few minutes, but that's the only choice you have today. I'm sorry."

"That's okay. I knew it was a long shot and I thank you for your trouble," and I turned to leave.

"Be careful," he said.

No kidding.

The way back up to the campus was the same as I had come down two hours earlier, except that it was uphill and was a lot longer. There were a few people on the streets, probably doing some necessary shopping before the fighting began again. It was starting to cloud up and the day had lost its early morning luster. It was lonely and depressing, and I knew it was time to climb up to Gordon's and listen to Wayland and Willie and some of the other good-old boys from home.

I got back to the campus with no problem and went to the cafeteria for lunch. Marcel was there with friends, and he motioned to me to meet him at the tennis court benches as soon as I had eaten. He was alone and waiting after I finished lunch, and I sat down rather heavily.

"No luck, I see," he said.

"Not for you either. I hope you won't have to move back any of my stuff you had your eye on."

"You told me to wait a couple of days before I moved anything, and I always do what you tell me to do."

"Yeah, right."

"My father called and said he'd be sending a car for us in the next day or two, but he doesn't know exactly when. He told us to be ready on a minute's notice. He means that literally."

"I can leave at anytime. I've got my toothbrush in my pocket now. I'm ready."

"Me too," said Marcel. "I'm sick of this place for a while. By the way, Joe said if I saw you to tell you there was going to be an important faculty meeting at Gordon's at 2:00 this afternoon. Your attendance is required. I told him you had gone to the American Embassy and that we might not ever see you again."

"Thanks."

"Don't mention it. If my father calls, I'll come and get you."

"Great. I shouldn't be hard to find."

That afternoon went like all the others at Gordon's, and the night on the stage went like four of the last five.

I was in my office the next morning when Marcel came by and said, "Let's go. The car will be at the South Gate in five minutes."

"I'm ready."

Outside it was raining like a son-of-a-bitch. There was no wind and it was coming straight down. Marcel had an umbrella, and we both got under it as best we could and ran for the gate. We were there in three minutes flat, but our driver was already there, standing outside in the rain, waiting for us. He opened the back door and, after we got in, ran around to the driver's side and got behind the wheel. He and Marcel talked about whatever and I kept silent. We drove about three minutes to a military station, which I often passed while walking to and from the university. The driver told us to wait in the car and he got out. It suddenly stopped raining, and we rolled the windows down to cool off and observe what was happening.

There were three white four-wheel-drive Range Rovers in a line and about ten Lebanese Army soldiers waiting to get in. Our driver called us to get out and motioned us to climb in the middle Rover, and we sat in the seat right behind the driver, with two armed guards squeezed in on either side of us. There was another guard behind us and one next to the driver. I noticed a Lebanese Army General getting into the Rover in front of us.

"We're lucky that such a high-ranking officer was going across today and that we could catch a ride with his convoy," I said.

"He's a decoy," Marcel said. "You and I are the reason everybody is going. Kind of makes you feel important, doesn't it? I told you my father was an influential man."

"Well, I'm impressed and grateful," I said, and I meant it.

The three Rovers pulled out of the small outpost and drove south for a kilometer and then turned to the east, toward the Shouf Mountains. The buildings were in ruins from the very heavy fighting, and the road guards who waved us through four or five checkpoints were steely-eyed, dirty, tired, and not smiling. I know that we passed through at least two or three districts of different militias' control, and we slowed down for nobody and no one attempted to stop us for any reason. To pull off a feat like that, Retired Interpol Colonel Abu Shakra must have had a great deal of influence indeed. Hell, the president of the country could not have done that. We made the trip with ease and passed over the Green Line to the other side at a place I had never seen before. It was located east of my everyday crossing at the National Museum, and it was at the beginning of the foothills to the mountains that rose above the city.

We bade goodbye to our armed guards and driver and thanked them for their good services. Marcel and I got in a waiting car, and the unarmed driver took us up into the mountains. It was the main road to Damascus, and although I lived on that very road, I had never followed it out of the city. Too risky. After we had traveled not more than two kilometers, we pulled up at an army checkpoint—a Syrian Army checkpoint. I had no idea that the Syrian Army was so close to the Lebanese capital city.

"Oh, yes," Marcel said. "My father's house is surrounded by Syrian artillery emplacements and a lot of Syrian soldiers."

It had suddenly become very cloudy and foggy as we entered the Syrian checkpost, but it did not start raining again. The guards knew the car and driver, and we passed through with no problem. Marcel's father's house was located in a dark green, heavily forested area, a few hundred yards farther up the mountain, and the entire area was quickly being obscured by the encroaching clouds of fog. We turned south off the main highway onto a smaller, private road and drove past a cannon battery with its long, gray barrels reaching up into the low-lying fog. The house was almost a hundred yards farther on, and the entire vicinity was enshrouded with fog, and visibility was perhaps forty yards. The house was very modern and made of dark gray concrete and glass. Except for the dark green conifers, the fog, house, and cannons produced a subdued, silent spectacle in gray that was fantastically surreal and just a little bit spooky.

We got out of the car and walked toward the house. We climbed an outdoor stairway to a large veranda on the second floor, where Marcel's father was waiting for us. He was seated outside in the fog and chill (the altitude was about two thousand feet), smoking a narghile, and he rose as we gained the veranda and walked across to greet him. He was not an imposing figure, perhaps 5'8", with a slim build and had a very kind, smiling face. He kissed Marcel and shook my hand. He spoke to me in French only, and I was polite as hell. Marcel translated for us both. After a few minutes, the housemaid called us to a late lunch, and we three sat down with Marcel's mother at the table and I ate my first home-cooked meal in a week. After lunch, I commented to Marcel on the unique taste of the kufteh, which is a very popular dish in many Lebanese homes. Somehow, it had a different taste.

"It's frozen," he said. "My mother's a terrible cook. By herself, she can't make anything worth eating. There is no one in the house to help her today."

Glad I brought it up.

That afternoon we relaxed at Marcel's beautiful home, and the most memorable thing that happened was the frigid shower I took. If that water had been half a degree colder, it would not have come out of the showerhead. Marcel showed me later—too late, of course—how to turn the hot water on. I'll get it right next time.

Early in the evening, Col. Abu Shakra himself drove me down to my house in the city. As I mentioned before, his home was on the same Damascus highway as mine, and it was a very short trip, perhaps fifteen minutes. It was all very pleasant despite his speaking in French the whole time. I listened well.

I particularly enjoyed the fact that this very powerful man, before whom all the toughest street fighters in West Beirut bowed, even if only for a short time, drove a small white Subaru. Now, that's style!

The Black Flags

As I came out of the west side checkpoint, on my way to the campus one morning, something told me not to take my normal route. Call it instinct, if you like, or a sixth sense, but I always listened to that inner voice and I know it has come in very useful on several occasions in my life.

The Amal Militia had taken over the Muslim West Side the week before, and I had spent a long, pleasant weekend at home with my family on the other side, and today was the first day I had returned to work since my escape from the campus, three days before. There was no fighting at that time, but I passed several tanks stationed on the way, which were surrounded by dirty, hard-looking fighters who did not seem to be in a very good mood. It seemed as if the color of choice for the Amal Militia was black. Black for death, I guess, and serious business in general. They had black flags at the tank emplacements, and they wore black armbands. Nobody was smiling, and I did not acknowledge their presence as I passed by. The service taxis were not running, and I had to walk the three or four kilometers to the university. I didn't mind the walk. I had done it many times, and I always left my house early enough to allow for emergencies of one kind or another.

My regular road from the main intersection at Barbir angled a bit toward the southwest, and after about two hundred meters, I turned off to the right to walk through a residential neighborhood that was, as the crow flies, a more direct route to the campus, but the streets were narrow and twisted and it was a good place to get lost, or worse. But I felt happy about my detour. It was very sunny and clear, most of the apartments and businesses were a bright ochre color that went well with the red, sandy soil, and it was a nice day, weather-wise.

My pleasant, optimistic mood was brought abruptly to a change when I saw, on a flat rooftop about fifty meters directly ahead of me, a long black flag waving back and forth, which was obviously a sinister signal of some kind. Was I to be captured and kidnapped? That was always a possibility and indeed was the fate of four of my university colleagues who were taken hostage after I had already left Beirut. (They were captured and held captive for four years.)

Perhaps my intuition had sent me the wrong way. I knew that I was a visible, well-known traveler back and forth across the Green Line, and I could have been picked up at almost anytime. Was today the day? I stopped and got out of the street and stepped up on the sidewalk to survey the situation and took a cigar out of my shirt pocket and fired it up. The black flag continued to wave by unseen hands. There was no person visible because of the high wall around the flat roof. It was very strange and a bit spooky. It was also very quiet, and I could have heard any approaching vehicle coming to get me, but there was no sound.

After three or four minutes, I continued on my journey and made it safely past the building with the flag on top. I had walked about fifty meters and pulled up short again. Just ahead of me was yet another black flag waving on top of another building and I figured my goose was cooked. They now had me located between the two flags and I was blocked off, front and rear, with no chance of escape through the walls or locked doors and windows of the buildings on either side of the street. I was trapped.

There was nothing to do but wait. On my right side, there was an indention between two buildings that offered a meager hiding place. It was a cul-de-sac that was wide enough for a car's passage but was only about thirty feet in length. There was a rusted-out car at the entrance, and I stepped quickly behind it and hoped for the best. As I waited, I noticed the car was riddled with bullet holes, especially on the driver's side, and I pitied the occupants who surely did not survive such an onslaught. There were perhaps seventy or eighty bullet holes in the small car, maybe more. Actually, there were abandoned cars like that all over Beirut, and I once asked some of my students to photograph me standing beside one such metallic corpse, but they refused.

Well, nothing happened. No cars or jeeps with screaming tires and armed militiamen came to get me. Nothing. I finished with my cigar and said to hell with it all. I had to move on to make it to my first class. Perhaps the cowboys got their directions mixed up or something. Anyway, it seemed as if today was not to be my day of demise, after all, and I walked briskly on my way and arrived at the university in good time. When I met my first class, I related the morning's experiences and how I had somehow escaped my would-be kidnappers, and every one of them burst out laughing.

"Professor Jack, that is so funny!" one of them finally blurted out.

"What's so damned funny about that?" I asked hotly. "I was completely helpless and it was pretty damned scary!"

"They weren't going to kidnap you," one said. "They were calling home their racing pigeons! Hah, hah, hah!" they all laughed.

"Well, I thought it was deadly serious," I said.

"It is deadly serious," one continued. "They bet big money on whose pigeons return home the fastest. They've been doing that for a thousand years!"

To Atlanta

During my one-year sojourn in Beirut, I was the artistic director and principal guest conductor of the Beirut Orpheus Choral Society. Due to the serious fighting, which often engulfed substantial portions of the city, we managed only two major concerts that year. The society members had wanted to produce an opera (or operetta, more likely), but putting on a staged production with orchestra was simply not practical and I said no. Such an undertaking would have taxed the musical resources of the entire city, and in spite of the fact that a deputy from the East German Embassy had promised me an orchestra whenever I needed one, it was seldom that the city was quiet enough for so many folks to meet at the same time and, more importantly, in the same location. There was no safe, neutral location.

In the Orpheus Chorus, there was a young Palestinian girl (young woman, actually), and on a couple of occasions after our rehearsals, she and I would go out for a drink at a nice bar on the main street in the Hamra district, just down the hill from the university campus. We would stay for thirty or forty minutes, and then she would walk home alone. After she would leave, if the city was quiet, I'd go home to East Beirut, and if not, I'd spend the night in my office. Her name was Ghada and she was very good-looking, charming, and smart. She was also a woman of great personal courage.

One Friday afternoon, as I was preparing to leave the campus, there was a knock on my office door and I called out, "Come in!"

The door opened, and in she walked. I was very surprised.

"Ghada! What are you doing here? What a pleasant surprise. How are you doing?"

"Fine," she said. "I've come to see you. Are you leaving now for the other side of the city?"

"Yes, I am, but there's no hurry. What can I do for you?"

"You can take me with you."

"Of course. When do you want to leave? The sooner, the better, you know."

"I know," she said. "I'm ready now."

She had a small bag over her shoulder and was wearing jeans and a casual shirt with jogging shoes.

"Well, I'm ready. Let's go."

I carried nothing. I always travel light, especially in Beirut.

We took a service taxi just outside the main gate and rode the three kilometers to the huge intersection at Barbir, which is the last stop before entering the Green Line Muslim Checkpoint at the museum crossing. We got out and began our passage through the very crowded market area, located within the intersection itself. Even in the best of times, it's a rough place to be, and we were pushed and jostled by vendors and buyers as we made our way across. I put my left arm around her waist and slipped my thumb through one of the belt loops in her jeans to hold her and keep her close. I didn't want to lose her. She was not a big girl, and it would have been easy for us to have become separated. The market area was so crowded that I didn't figure anyone would notice or object to my western familiarity, but we were still on the Muslim side and had to be careful. I knew that Palestinians had to be careful, no matter what. I had once witnessed a Palestinian fellow dragged out of my service taxi to the sidewalk and murdered on the spot because he was Palestinian. Maybe it was for some other reason, but that's what the driver told me, anyway. I didn't want that happening to Ghada. Nevertheless, after we had progressed through most of the market and intersection, she removed my arm from around her waist and instead got behind me and grabbed onto my heavy belt with one hand and let me pull her through the rest of the way. It worked, and we came out of the rough and madding crowd unscathed.

From the intersection it was less than a hundred meters to the checkpoint and as we approached, I noticed a guy who was sitting in a new position on a stool in the middle of the passageway. The passageway was simply the existing street, and the checkpoint had a small guardhouse about ten meters to the right side, and .50-caliber machinegun emplacements were barricaded on either side, with armed guards who, most of the time, were drinking coffee. I must say that the guards on both sides were always friendly and courteous to me. I never had a problem at the checkpoints; it was the 800-meter stretch in between that could be unpleasant at times.

The guy on the stool was facing the other direction as we walked by, and as I had already nodded to some of the fellows I knew, I ignored him, which he obviously did not like. We had gone a few steps past him and he said something, which I also ignored.

Ghada smiled up at me and said, "He wants you to stop."

I kept walking and replied, "I'm sorry, but I don't understand the language."

Then I heard the bolt of an automatic rifle drawn back and released. Now, that was a language I did understand.

We stopped and turned around and the kid—he was sixteen or seventeen years old—gave a tiny motion with his right hand for me to come back. He remained seated with his AK-47 lying across his lap, and he didn't move as we returned to stand before him. He made another motion with his hand and I gave him my university ID, which I had already been taking out of my pocket. He looked at me from under his hat brim, and I have never, before or since, seen such mean, yellow eyes that burned with undisguised hatred. He wanted to kill me. I was very cordial and smiled, and I think he didn't like it that I was not afraid of him or his gun.

One of the regulars came over and spoke to the killer and then spoke to me in English. "Please come inside. The captain wants to see you."

We all walked into the guardhouse, and the captain in charge wished me a good afternoon and then, Ghada told me later, he told the kid that I passed through every day and it wasn't necessary to check my ID. In front of the kid, he apologized for disturbing us and wished us a safe journey across. I thanked him and assured him that we had suffered no inconvenience whatsoever, and we wished him and his men a safe and pleasant weekend. We left the guardhouse, and I never saw the mean kid again.

On our way across, Ghada said, "I think that boy wanted to kill you."

"No question about it. I think it's a good thing he's surrounded by reasonably level-headed grown men. You've got to watch out for the teenagers. They'll kill you in a second and not think about it. Killing people is a child's game, and any fifteen-year-old with a gun can do it well. Grown men are not so dangerous."

We made it across without further incident and after we passed through the East Checkpoint, I asked her where she wanted to go. "I have a taxi driver who is always first in line if I need him, and he will take you anywhere you want to go."

"I want to go with you," she said. "Or rather, I want you to go with me," she corrected.

"Where are you going?"

"To Atlanta," she said with a perfectly straight face.

"Atlanta, Georgia?" I asked. "Now?"

"That's right," she said. "Tonight."

"Well, I can't go with you to Atlanta. I have a wife and two children and could not leave them, even for such an attractive proposition."

"Oh, I didn't mean for you to go all the way to Atlanta, just go far enough to help me leave Lebanon. President Salibi said that you are a nice man and that you would help me."

"The president (of the university) said that about me? Is he a friend of yours?"

"For many years," she said. "He was a friend of my father's."

"Uh-huh. Do you have your passport with you?"

"No. Palestinians don't have passports."

"Do you have permission to leave the country? Has your father written an affidavit for you?"

At that time, for any Lebanese woman to leave the country, she had to have her father's or her husband's permission.

"No, no, my father, uncles, and brothers have all been killed. There are no men left in my family."

"I see," I said. "Only me."

"Yes," she smiled sweetly. "Only you."

Reminded me of an old Roy Orbison tune.

"So, you're going to sneak out of the country."

"Yes, with your help, I hope. Let's go have a cup of coffee and talk it over."

An excellent idea.

It was a plan straight out of a movie thriller. She was to be at a certain point on the shore between Beirut and Jounieh at midnight. She was to signal out to sea with a flashlight, and a small, fast boat would come close to the shore, pick her up, and take her to Cypress. She described the pickup point to me, and if her description was correct, I knew it well.

During the warm weather of the previous late summer and early fall, I had often driven there to go swimming, and it was about the most hospitable place for beach activities located between the two cities. The beach was rather small and rocky but relatively flat, and one could have a picnic there, throw a Frisbee, pitch a tent, or whatever. It wasn't perfect and was not too comfortable, but it was probably the best place to go for a swim. The rest of the shoreline was predominantly one hundred/one hundred-fifty foot cliffs— beautiful, but not practical for swimming. It had to be the place for her midnight rendezvous.

"Can you swim?"

"Yes," she replied simply.

"Have you been there before?"

"No, but friends of mine were there two weeks ago, and they said it looked okay and they gave me a map."

"That's good. And can you find the way down the cliffs in the dark?" I asked.

"Can you?" she countered.

"If it's the place where I go swimming, I can do it."

"Then so can I," she said.

I had been to the place perhaps twenty times, and I had never seen anyone there besides me. As long as there were no cowboys about, the operation should be relatively simple and maybe even easy. If there happened to be other folks around, or some Phalangist fighters holed up there, or other smugglers like me, well, that would complicate matters a great deal and probably render the mission impossible.

The rendezvous point was about twenty minutes' driving time north of Bourj Hammoud, and Ghada and I arranged to meet at the traffic circle in Sin-El-Fil, close to my house. I needed to go home and see my family, if they weren't at the mountain house, and rest up for the evening's adventures. I also needed to eat dinner. There was no telling how long it would take to get her on the boat and off to Cypress. In addition, I needed to change to dark clothes and lightweight shoes for swimming. We agreed to meet at 10:00 to take a service taxi to Bourj Hammoud and meet my Armenian driver, whom my wife would call in the meantime, at my usual place, the large intersection with the white van. While I was at home, Ghada would have dinner with a friend of hers and pick up a powerful flashlight.

At just a few minutes before 10:00, with my binoculars case looped over my shoulder, I left the house and walked to the traffic circle. Ghada was already there and was carrying a small shopping bag, which I assumed contained the flashlight. We hailed a service and climbed in the back. It took five to ten minutes to reach our appointed intersection, and we paid the driver and got out. Arto had not yet shown up, and we waited near the white van.

"You care for a beer?" I asked. "That white van is loaded with hooch at very cheap prices. I'm a favored customer."

"Really?" she laughed. "But no thanks. Maybe later."

Later? Maybe she meant thirty years down the line.

"Hello, Mr. Jack!" Arto had come up behind us without my noticing him. "Good evening. Your wife called me and said I was to take you and your girlfriend anywhere you wanted to go and that she would pay me big, big money!" he said with a big, big grin. "I sure wish I had an understanding wife like that!"

"She's the best," I said. "And she can sing."

"Big money and sweet singing. Some people have all the luck. Where are we going?" he added as he motioned us down the street toward his car.

I did not introduce Ghada.

"North, towards Jounieh."

"My favorite city," he said.

I didn't ask why.

We got in his car with Ghada in the back. I rode shotgun. Speaking of shotguns, actually, I would have liked to have had a shotgun along. Shotguns are comforting at almost anytime and any occasion (perhaps not bridal showers, but just about everywhere else). Although most of the tough guys in the movies and on TV use pump guns, I always preferred a five-shot automatic myself, with big-old fat double-ought buckshot—heavy on the powder. The best thing about shotguns is, if you're scared shitless and your knees are banging together like castanets, and your hands are shaking, you can still probably hit your target. Am I digressing?

It was a short drive up the main road to Jounieh, and it followed the spectacular Mediterranean coastline. Two or three miles out of the city, we passed the notorious smugglers' wharf and pier, which jutted out some one hundred meters into the sea. That was a dangerous place, and the Phalangist guards there brooked no trespassing of any kind whatsoever, and to be caught snooping around those premises would be a fatal mistake. The pier was completely dark at that time. There was not a light of any kind to be seen, although I knew there were plenty of caretakers around waiting on the next shipment of smuggled, stolen goods that would be sold on the black markets throughout the country, thus helping to support Christian causes in Lebanon.

Just before the second exit past the pier, Ghada recognized a building from her friend's description, and she old Arto to turn off the main highway and take the small road, which would curve underneath the highway at the next bridge and take us to the edge of the high cliffs above the sea. Arto and I both knew the area, and her pickup point was indeed my summertime swimming locale. We pulled off to the west side of the small road onto a level gravel area, which had room enough for two or three cars, and Arto killed the engine and turned out the headlights.

We got out of the car and stepped carefully over to the edge of the cliff and looked down. My eyes were not yet adjusted to the dark, of course, but it was easy to see the whitewater waves as they hit against the shore about one hundred fifty feet below. Approximately ten or fifteen yards off the shore, there was a strange, rather fascinating rock formation that I called the shark's teeth. They were in a straight line running parallel to the shore and resembled the teeth on the blade of a crosscut saw more than shark's teeth (I think). There were five or six of them in the formation sticking up about ten or twelve feet out of the water. The "teeth" were wide at the water's level and tapered to relatively sharp points at the top. They were positioned about six feet apart, wide enough to swim through, but too narrow for even a small boat to pass through without risk. Ghada would have to swim past the rock formation, perhaps fifteen or twenty yards, for the boat to have room enough to pick her up safely.

There was a steep gravel road leading down to the beach that was passable for a four-wheel-drive vehicle, but not for Arto's car. I wanted to go on foot anyway. We had arrived in plenty of time for me to go down alone and check out the situation before Ghada would make her descent. I told them both to wait at the top and that I would return quickly, I hoped. Much of the natural rocks and gravel were loose and slippery, and I had to be very careful as I went down. My eyes were slowly becoming adjusted to the darkness, and I managed to get down without breaking my neck.

There was no one at the bottom, just as I had expected, and if Ghada survived the climb down the cliffs and the short sea swim, she would be able to board her boat for freedom—if it showed up. I had my doubts about that, but I kept them to myself.

I climbed back up the road, and it was somewhat easier than going down. I got Ghada and her small shoulder bag and flashlight and told Arto that his work was done and he could go back to the city, that he and his car didn't need to be parked in such a strange, suspicious location in the middle of the night. He protested mildly but eventually agreed.

"How will you get home?" he asked.

"I haven't thought that far ahead yet," I said. "Probably walk. It's not far."

"This is not a safe place for you to be, out on the road at night."

"It's not safe for you either," I said, "and that's why you need to go home."

"Yeah, but you're a foreigner."

"Shit, so are you. You damned Armenian."

"Okay, okay," he laughed. "I'll meet you at the white van when you get back, and I'll buy you a beer for breakfast. What's your brand?"

"Ararat, of course," I said.

"Of course. I had forgotten." And he got in his car and drove off.

I turned to Ghada. "Let's go. We still have about forty-five minutes, but it's better to be early. We'll find a place about halfway down to sit and wait. Trying to signal with the flashlight from the shore might not work. Those rocks just off shore may block their view. The light does work, doesn't it?"

"It words very well," she said.

"Be careful with all the small rocks and gravel. You could break a leg here very easily."

As we went down together, it became obvious that the legs broken that night wouldn't be hers. She was as agile and sure-footed as a black Spanish goat, and I needed to take care of myself only. We found a place just off the narrow road that would give us some shelter from the road and allow an unrestricted view of the sea. My field glasses were the very best, and we would be able to see them well when they were a few miles offshore. How far the light could be seen from shore, I had no idea, but I knew that ours would be the only light for two kilometers, north and south. After dark, the Lebanese countryside became almost black. There were no highway lights and very few lights of any kind between Beirut and Jounieh. There was no electric power. I mean, it was dark out there, almost as dark as the Romanian countryside after the sun goes down. We sat together and waited.

"What are you taking with you?" I asked. "That's a pretty small bag for such a long journey. Got any money?"

"Very little. The organization that provides the boat to Cypress will give me money, a passport, and a ticket to Atlanta. I don't have to take anything with me."

"Nice organization."

"Very nice," she said. "And if this goes well, they may ask you to assist some more Palestinian women in the future. Would you do that?"

"Are they all as beautiful as you?"

"More beautiful," she said.

"You bet! By the way, do you like Coca Cola?"

"Huh?"

"Atlanta is famous being the headquarters of Coca Cola. You'll have to drink a Coke from time to time. Just like I drink Ararat beer in Bourj Hammoud. It's smart business. It's patriotic. It might save your life."

"Oh, I like Coca Cola just fine, but I prefer beer."

"Well, they've got beer in Atlanta, too. Don't worry."

With my field glasses, I searched the sea and every place I could check out on the shore below, and we seemed to be completely alone. At ten minutes before midnight, I told her to take out the flashlight and send out a three-dot signal due west of our position and then to the northwest as well. Never having done this before, I didn't really know what a proper signal might be, but it was time. Just because I couldn't see a boat from our vantage point did not necessarily mean that there wasn't one out there—or maybe two or three. I certainly hoped we didn't signal to the wrong boat. The area was rife with smugglers—real smugglers, not amateurs like me—and they would not be playing games. But I hoped the professionals were five miles back toward Beirut, where they were supposed to be. Ghada said her boat would signal with a blinking red light and then switch to green when they got close to the shore. She continued signaling at one-minute intervals.

At two minutes after midnight, there was a red signal light from almost due west, about four miles out—maybe less. It was very exciting. Ghada jumped up, grabbed her bag, and handed me the flashlight. I told her to sit back down for two or three more minutes and continue signaling. I was as excited as she was. I watched through my glasses and observed what I thought was a rather large boat, perhaps too large for our friends. But as I waited, I saw a smaller boat, about twenty-five feet in length, come from behind the larger boat and head in our direction. There were three men on board, and I'd seen enough.

"Let's go. Walk slowly. We have plenty of time."

She was up and away, but I caught her and made her hold hands with me as we stumbled down to the shore. I needed the help.

We sent one last signal just before we reached the flat beach area, which was pretty well blocked from the sailors' view by the shark teeth formation. We walked quickly to the water's edge and peered through the gaps between the rocks. The sea was louder and rougher than I had anticipated, but the rocky teeth managed to break the waves coming to the shore. Outside the rocks...we'd just have to manage. I sent another quick signal just in case they were able to see us and was rewarded by a green signal light not one hundred yards offshore.

I took her bag and told her to swim to the tooth directly in front of us. There was a ledge underneath the water that a person could stand on, and I told her to wait for me there. She walked in and started swimming immediately, because the water got very deep just a few feet from shore. I left my binoculars and the flashlight on the beach and draped her bag strap around my neck and followed her. The water was a bit nippy, but not bad. She had reached the rock's ledge easily and waited for me until I caught up with her. We looked around the shoulder of the rock and saw the boat, maintaining its position about twenty yards distant. The men were motioning for her to come on and she took off, swimming like an otter. I followed with her bag and made sure the waves did not push her back onto the rocks. The boat ventured a bit closer, and two of the men reached down to grab her arms and pull her out of the water. While still in the water, I took the strap from around my neck and handed it to one of the men and then pushed away from the boat. Ghada leaned to the side of the boat and waved. I know she said thanks, but the sudden roar of the boat's engine and the crashing of the waves against the rocks covered up her voice. And then she was gone.

I swam back easily and slipped between two of the shark's teeth to the calmer waters close to the shore. When I was able to touch bottom, I climbed with short steps onto the beach and shook myself like a dog. After a short rest, I picked up my binoculars and the light and started up the rocky road to the top of the cliffs. I resisted the urge to use the light to help me find my way, because I could see well enough and the light might attract unwanted attention. At the top, I sat down for a few minutes to catch my breath. All of a sudden, I was very tired. Even without any hostile interference, my efforts in getting Ghada to the boat had been more strenuous and stressful than I had realized. In all fairness, I wasn't a young man anymore, even so long ago, and it had been a long day that wasn't over yet.

Now I was faced with the long walk back to the city in wet clothes. The weather was pleasantly warm, and my clothes would probably dry out by the time I got back. I stood up and got started. As I did so, I heard a car engine start up behind me, and I was suddenly caught in the headlights of a car that quickly pulled even with me and the passenger door opened.

"Want a ride, Mr. Jack?" Arto's voice called out.

"Don't mind if I do. What took you so long to pick me up? I must have walked at least twenty yards."

"Sorry about that," he said. "I know important people like you are used to fast, efficient service, but I did my best."

"You did well," I declared. "Let's get the hell out of here!"

Arto dropped me off in Bourj Hammoud, and I declined his breakfast beer offer. It was too early, or maybe too late; look at it any way you want.

I took a service back home and climbed the stairs to my fourth-floor apartment and went inside. Everyone was fast asleep, of course. I took a hot shower and went into the living room to enjoy a comfortable chair and a stiff glass of Ireland's best before I went to bed. After that, I went into the bedroom to join my sweet wife, who always sang so well.

Tanks and Frisbees

Behind my apartment in Sin-El-Fil, there was a small tank installation, which contained eight or ten of the monster machines and enough men to service them. It was actually only a short block away. If you turned left as you went out my front door, walked down the hill about thirty meters, and turned left again and proceeded another thirty meters up the hill, you'd be there. The entrance was on the corner, and the post took up less than half a block. It was quite unimpressive, really, until you saw the tanks parked inside.

One Saturday morning, my five-year-old daughter, Gabriella, and I took our Frisbee up there and were tossing it back and forth on the relatively flat area around the entrance to the outpost. A couple of the guys came out and asked to join us, and we cordially agreed. They were just boys, perhaps seventeen or eighteen years old, and weren't very good at it. They probably had never seen a Frisbee before. But it didn't matter; they had a great time running and throwing, and a few others came out to join us as well. Gabriella and I pretty much stopped participating and let the fellows enjoy playing with the Frisbee. They were a bit rough about it all, and we stayed prudently out of the way.

After about half an hour, we told the soldiers that we had to go home and we'd come back on the morrow. While we had been sitting out and watching, Gabriella and I had discussed giving the Frisbee to the fellows so they could play every day, and we could come and visit at anytime and play with them. She agreed, and as we were leaving we told them to keep the Frisbee. They protested loudly but, after a few short seconds, accepted our gift with much enthusiasm. They asked where we lived, and I pointed out the back veranda of our fourth-story apartment, and they nodded and one said whenever we needed anything, "And I mean anything," he reiterated, "don't hesitate to call on us." He meant it.

Gabriella and I walked back down to our place and we both felt happy about our visit, she with her generosity, and I, with having acquired a few very heavy-hitting friends who could, and would, give us a hand if and when the need arose.

I don't know about how you feel, but having a couple of friendly tanks in your neighborhood-watch program can be very comforting, especially in a city like Beirut.

California Crossing

Going back to the Christian side early one afternoon, I was crossing the Green Line, and as I passed through the Muslim Checkpoint, I was stopped by a shout. "Hey! Where are you going?" It was a friendly tone, for a change.

I stopped and turned to my left and saw a guy, armed with an AK-47, checking the cars as they passed over to the other side. For a few days, both sides had allowed cars to pass through, and there was no longer only pedestrian traffic.

"I'm going home," I answered as I walked over to him. I had never seen him before at the checkpoint. He was a newfer.

"Where are you from?" he asked in perfect American English.

"I'm from Texas," I said.

"What are you doing here?" he asked.

There were no cars passing through, and we had time to chat a moment. I figured he was from LA. He was about twenty-six, of medium height, had a big smile and a neatly trimmed black beard, and he was very handsome and just a little bit dangerous. He was smart. He knew what he was doing, and I knew he had come over to Beirut to help out with the killing. He volunteered to be here. Like me, I guess, come to think of it.

"I'm teaching at BUC," I said.

"Great. But why here?"

"My wife's hometown," I said, "and maybe I'm a little bit crazy."

"Hey!" he shouted with a big smile, "me too!"

Crazy as hell, I thought. He *was* a little bit crazy.

I turned and started to continue on my way. "See you tomorrow," I said.

"Hey, wait a minute and I'll get you a ride."

"Oh, I don't mind walking. I do it every day," I said.

"Hold on a second," he said as he stopped the next approaching car.

He stuck his AK-47 in the driver's window, about four inches from his face, and spoke a few quick words in Arabic.

"Hop in the back. They're glad to give you a ride over."

Sure they are, delighted.

I felt sorry for them—an old man and his wife who were probably scared shitless to be driving across in the first place, and who were now having to give a ride to a complete stranger who would probably murder them before they reached the other side. They were not happy to give me a ride, but what could they do? The friendly, handsome guy with the rifle told them to do it and if they refused or put up a fuss, he might kill them—in a friendly sort of way, of course. I wasn't happy to be in a car either. I felt much safer going across on foot, and the car was a huge target. Riding in the back seat of the car was a very bad idea in every way I could think of, but I climbed in for the same reason that they agreed to take me along.

"Thanks." I smiled and waved to the guy from southern California.

We drove slowly along the road, careful not to run over the pedestrians or fall in a shell hole. The road was straight and in fairly good condition, considering the intense fighting over the past two or three months. Heck, the war had been going on for years, and there was no road in Beirut that was in good condition.

The woman started talking to her husband, and I realized they were Armenian. I told them my wife was Armenian and that I took Armenian lessons from the Catholicos at the large church just north of Bourj Hammoud. Well, after that, they were indeed happy to give me a ride. They were positively jubilant to have me in their car. (Not really, they were just so glad that I probably was not going to kill them. We Armenians stick together.) They were very relieved and offered to take me anywhere I wanted to go, but I declined and said that I would get out before we got to the eastern checkpoint. About fifty meters before the checkpoint, I got out of the car and walked the rest of the way. They were safer traveling alone, and so was I. Much safer.

They drove up to the checkpoint, and the guards there questioned them a minute or two and looked in the trunk, long enough for me to catch up with them and lean in on the wife's side and tell them thanks. They smiled and waved (they meant it, this time), and we went our separate ways.

Downtown Poker

One Sunday afternoon, my wife and mother-in-law and I left the shop in Bourj Hammoud and were driving home to our apartment in Sin El Fil. I was driving our old slant, six-cylinder '65 Dodge sedan and the ladies were in the back, shouting at each other and at me (mainly), and I was not in a good mood. The old Dodge was newly-painted white, with new, red upholstery and, like all old Dodges, almost completely bulletproof—an attractive feature in Beirut. The car was perfect for that city. It was in excellent running condition, it looked fine, but it was too old and too slow for someone to want to steal it. If you drove a nice car in Beirut, you had to be prepared to kill to keep it. I am not joking.

Anyway, we were driving through a small outdoor market down a very narrow one-way street, which zigged and zagged in between various stalls and wagons of the street vendors, when we were met head-on by a man driving a very fast BMW, with lights flashing and his left arm waving out the window with his fingertips pressed together, a Beirut custom indicating I should stop and back up to let him pass. I was going in the proper direction and he was breaking the law. (What law?) Normally, I would back up in such a situation, but this time I was pissed off with the women in the back seat and as I looked in the rearview mirror, I noticed a car inching up behind me. It was going to be impossible for me to back up. Well, maybe not impossible, but it was going to be difficult.

The women continued shouting, and I got out of the car and started to stride over to the BMW to read the driver a few lines from the Good Book. He got out, too.

"Look out!" my mother-in-law shouted. "He's got a gun!"

"Good!" I shouted back. "He's going to need one!" I used to be tough. Texas tough. Besides, I had an ace in the hole. My mother-in-law's voice would stop a bullet in mid-air. No problem.

Now, as I have mentioned earlier, a BMW was one of those cars that owners had to be willing to kill to keep. That thought crossed my mind as I marched from my car to his. He was carrying a pistol on his hip but indicated no intention of using it.

"You're going the wrong way on this street," I said to him with some force.

From his uniform, I realized he was a Lebanese soldier, not a militiaman. He was a young officer, about twenty-five years old, spoke excellent English, and had some manners, thank God.

"I know," he said, "but I'm in a hurry."

"Well, I don't think I can back up now," I answered, indicating the cars that had come up behind me.

"You're right, of course. My mistake," he said, and he returned to his car and backed up enough to let us through.

As I drove by, I wanted to ask him if he would like to trade cars. I would have thrown in my mother-in-law to sweeten the pot, but I don't think he was in the mood for such tomfoolery. You've got to know when to hold and know when to fold, and I figured I had used up enough good luck for one day, so I cashed in my chips and retired from the field. I kept my mouth shut and drove straight on home while I was still ahead in the game.

The Flower Girl

Crossing the Green Line, the no-man's land between the Muslim West and Christian East Beirut, was a routine that I performed almost every day. I lived on the Christian side, and every morning I went to work on the Muslim side and returned home around mid-afternoon. Normally, the later one waited to cross back over in either direction, the more dangerous it became. I always assumed that the cowboys awoke from their naps around 2:00 or 3:00 and started getting into mischief soon thereafter.

One weekday afternoon, after my last class, some of my students had treated me to a short drink at one of the waterholes near the campus, and one of my favorite students, Micheline, had given me a single red rose to take with me back to the other side. I took it with pleasure, of course, and carried it in my hand as I crossed through the Muslim Checkpoint and began my eight hundred-yard trek past the deserted Hippodrome to the other side.

There were several others making the same journey, the sun was shining, the folks were smiling, and it looked to be one of those afternoons when the crossover would be as pleasant as a stroll through the Prater in Vienna.

After I had gone about halfway, someone opened up with a .50-caliber machinegun and started sending those heavy rounds most definitely in my direction (and others', too) and with the practiced ease of a veteran Beirut native, I hit the dirt. From past experience and keen observation, I knew all the safe places to take cover throughout the entire length of the crossing, and I knew that the best and closest place to weather the present storm was a shallow depression immediately on my right and just a few yards in front of me. It was about two feet deep and long enough to accommodate a man of my size. I dived head first into the shallow hole and scrunched, belly down, into the soft, sandy red dirt at the bottom. The relatively slow thumps of the .50-caliber continued, and I could not imagine why someone was using such a heavy weapon, when a .30-caliber would have worked just as well, maybe better, and a lot cheaper.

While I was considering these practical thoughts, I was suddenly jarred by the impact of someone else piling in on top of me in the tiny space. I could not see who it was, but two smooth, slim arms wrapped themselves around my neck and the wonderful, sweet scent of some feminine perfume, and the long, black hair that cascaded around my head left no doubt that a young woman had joined me in the narrow, shallow ditch.

I knew that the small depression was too shallow for her to be safe from the continuing machinegun fire, so I turned on my side to put my body between her and the machinegun, which was firing from the west, and rolled her off me onto her side to the east portion of our scanty shelter. We were then face to face, at a distance of about a sixteenth of an inch. If we had been any closer, I would have been on the other side of her. At that distance it was hard to be sure, but she seemed to be very pretty, about twenty years old, and her eyes were almost smiling.

"Merci beaucoup," she said.

"De rien," I replied. (Joe Cool)

"Vous etes un gentleman et un cavalier."

"Bien sur."

She stopped talking, thank God, because I had pretty well exhausted my French. At that time, I realized that I was still holding in my right hand the flower Micheline had given me, and as best I could, I brought it between the girl's face and mine and asked her, "Voulez-vous une fleur?"

Such a look she gave me! Actually, I couldn't see it too well, but I could feel it.

"Oui. Absolument!" she declared, and I passed it two inches into her hand.

I wanted to sing a few bars from "The Flower Song" from "Carmen," but we were too close together for me to breathe properly, and it wasn't necessary. She loved it.

We waited patiently, and after a few more minutes the firing stopped and I stuck my head up to check out the situation. Others were coming out from behind walls and trees and out of holes like ours, and it seemed safe enough to continue on our respective journeys. Unfortunately, she was going the opposite direction from me, and she smiled and thanked me again and left.

I dusted off my clothes, passed through the East Checkpoint, and nodded to the guards as I walked through. They laughed and appeared to be glad that I was not injured, and I don't think anybody had been hurt. Maybe the cowboys just wanted to practice their shooting and watch all of us dive for cover. Who knows?

Three or four weeks later, as I was beginning to cross over the Green Line, an attractive young woman spoke to me as we passed. Beirutis are very friendly, but she had warmth in her greeting that was out of the ordinary.

"Bonjour, monsieur. Comment t'allez vous?" she said, and I greeted her in my friendliest French but was almost to the far checkpoint before I realized that she was the flower girl from the earlier crossing.

Perhaps we passed each other by on several occasions, but I don't recollect seeing her again. It was a wonderful encounter, and I hope she remembers me as fondly as I remember her.

Moos

When I first arrived in Korea, I worked at an English institute in Gumi, and when my boss was showing me around my new apartment, he indicated I could buy what food I needed at the "supermarket" just across the small parking lot. After he left, I looked out the fifth-floor windows on the veranda and there was no supermarket to be seen, at least as far as I could tell. After a few days, I found it, exactly where he said it was, except there was nothing "super" about it. It was about the size of a large walk-in closet and a lot more crowded. You could get in the store just fine, but you had to back out the front door to turn around and then slide sideways back inside to see what was on the other side of the aisle. I exaggerate a little, but not much.

One weekend, I fancied some breakfast cereal to start the day and realized that I had no milk. I put on a heavy coat and my hat and marched down to the supermarket. At that time, I did not know the Korean word for milk, and I said slowly, in my very best English, "I would like some milk, please."

His eyes glazed over, and I repeated the question and he walked immediately to the back of the store and returned with a couple of bottles of beer.

"No, thank you," I said, and then asked for milk in a couple of other languages, to no avail.

I walked around the store and saw nothing that looked like milk. But I did see a small stool, and with the owner watching me closely, I sat down on the stool, took off my cowboy hat, and placed it upside down between my knees. I then made cow-milking motions with my hands and, with my mouth, the *swish, swish, swish, swish* sounds of alternating streams of milk shooting through the foam on top and into the bucket of milk below. It was a demonstration only an expert could have done, and I looked up at him expectantly. Nothin'. He was a city boy and had probably never seen a cow! By that time, two young women had come into the store and they were laughing behind their hands. They knew exactly what I wanted but did not offer to help out. They were probably too shy. They had probably never seen a foreigner before, and he had never seen a cow. Life can be difficult in a foreign country, I tell you.

Finally, in desperation, I cupped my hands around my mouth and in my stentorian, operatic baritone voice produced a moo that would have made the finest Jersey cow in Palo Pinto County very proud indeed.

"Oo Yoo!" the store owner shouted and went back to a cooler I had not noticed and returned with two liters of milk.

I slapped my money on the counter, picked up the change and my hard-earned milk, and went to the house.

Living in a foreign country and dealing with a foreign culture can be challenging, and sometimes you have to be very creative to get what you want. It is not for the faint of heart. If you're lucky and keep your eyes and mind open, a new adventure may be awaiting you just around every corner. But before you set sail for foreign lands, practice your moos. You may be glad you did.

Straight Talk

In Gumi, I had what is called a split shift. I taught professional folks for an hour starting at 6:30 a.m., before they went to work, and school children after school until in the early evening. The institute had a medium-sized bus that drove around to pick me up and several students as well. Sometimes I would walk, but most of the time I took the bus. On our way, we often stopped at the bottom of a small hill to wait for a very cute student who was always late. She would stumble out of a side street about forty yards up the hill and run down to the bus carrying a coat and bag, with other stuff, perhaps an umbrella, all in disarray, and would climb in the bus out of breath, nodding and smiling to all the passengers. She always wore a hat or cap and had a dynamite smile. She would sit with friends at the front of the bus and visit during the five-minute ride to the institute. She was not a student in any of my classes, and I did not know her name.

After I had taught at the institute about six months, as I was preparing to leave my classroom for the day, she came into my room with one of my older female students who spoke English quite well.

"Jack," my student said, "this is a good friend of mine, and she wants you to go with her to the theater to see a show. She doesn't speak English very well, and she wanted me to ask you. The show is called 'DMZ' and it's tomorrow night at 7:30. It's a live performance."

I looked at the girl and she gave me a terrific smile and nodded.

"I would love to go," I said, and I meant it, "but I have one rule in my life that I keep, and it's that I never go out on a date with my students. I realize that she is not in one of my classes, but she is a student here at the institute and I'm sorry, but I must decline her very attractive request."

My student translated for her, and I watched as the girl immediately turned around and walked out of the room and down the hall to the reception desk and talked to the secretary there for about ten or fifteen seconds and then returned. She spoke a few words to my student and my student said, "She has just quit studying here. Now, will you go?"

Now, I'm not the smartest person in the world, but even I could figure that out.

"I believe I will," I said. I was impressed. I'm still impressed, fifteen years later.

We went to see "DMZ" (a staged musical, not a rock group, thank God), and we've been going to the theater ever since. She's in my house at this very moment, singing in the room next to my study.

Chips on Sunday

When my wife decided that she and I would become one couple, she thought I needed to go to church. I wanted to please her and agreed, as long as we didn't overdo it. She agreed in turn, and if memory serves me right, we visited once or twice a month at a small protestant church located about half a block from my apartment. The folks there were very nice and were my neighbors, and it didn't hurt my standing in the community for them to see me coming to church with my cute, young Korean wife. In addition, there were two other positive things about the church service: I did not understand one word of the entire affair, and while scrunched down in the pew, I took up the reading of Kafka, which I understood a good deal better.

We always sat over halfway back and on the left side. (That's the stage-right side for you theater people.) One morning, before the service started, my wife was chatting with some of the church members and I was seated alone on our customary pew and reading my book. All of a sudden, two very cute girls, perhaps six or seven years old, came across the aisle and sat down quite close to me and were smiling and laughing and having a very good time in general. They were eating potato chips and somehow were excited about, well, I didn't know what. At the same time, each of them offered me a potato chip. Now, I like pretty girls and I like potato chips, and I could tell this was going to be a very enjoyable Sunday morning, although I couldn't help but feel that something was not quite right. For one thing, most children in Korea give me a wide berth. These young ladies were almost aggressive and were hustling me. Had they been a few years older, I would have checked my wallet, just to be on the safe side. I've been to Waco and three county fairs, and very friendly young ladies who are not known to me tend to make me nervous, although the potato chips were comforting.

I reached for one of the chips and just as I was about to take it, she drew it away, laughing and shaking her head in a "no" sort of way. Perhaps I had made a mistake and should have taken the other one first. They continued to smile and laugh, and I attempted to take the other proffered chip, but with the same result. I looked at them in question and opened my hands, palms up, and shrugged my shoulders, indicating I didn't understand what I was supposed to do. They both pointed at my chest. I looked down and thought maybe I had been drooling (something I have done in church on several occasions) or I had a button undone, or whatever. Hell, I didn't know. I could see nothing amiss. I raised my head to look at them again, and the closest girl got up on her knees and touched my shirt pocket. Ah-ha! I got it! Inside my shirt pocket was a package of gum. I took it out and they both nodded very enthusiastically and, with huge grins, held out the chips again. I was right. This had been a set-up all along and had nothing to do with Christian charity. They wanted to trade their potato chips for my gum. The old man finally figured it out.

Well, I bought it. I took out two pieces of gum, one in each hand, and offered them to the girls. They reached for them greedily, but just as they had almost grabbed them, I quickly pulled my hands back, just as they had done to me. For a split second they were shocked and upset but laughed again as I pointed at the single chip each one had, shook my head, and indicated more chips instead of just one. They nodded their heads in agreement and added a substantial handful of chips to complete the deal. They gave me the chips, took the gum, and returned to their former places across the aisle. Everyone was satisfied. I can't remember when I ever had a better time in church.

Country Kosen

Song Jeong Ri is a small town located just three or four kilometers southwest of Gwang ju. It has perhaps ten or fifteen thousand inhabitants and is quite provincial in just about every way you can think of. I liked the town and would often ride my bicycle over there from the university, a distance of about two kilometers. I lived on campus and the narrow, concrete country road, which ran along the river for about half the distance, and then through flat rice fields, offered a welcome respite from my teaching duties and the busy campus life.

For almost a year, on Saturdays, I had a part-time job at an English institute in the town, and I taught children ranging in ages from eight to thirteen or fourteen. My classes lasted two hours, I enjoyed them a lot, and I always rode my bike.

My bike, although almost new at that time, was a bit old-fashioned in that it had wheel fenders, a sprocket guard, and a comfortable seat on which I could deposit my skinny behind. The handlebars were positioned so that I could ride sitting straight up, not crouched over for maximum speed and minimum wind drag. I was never in a hurry and it was a bike I could, and often did, ride while wearing a coat and tie. It was a gentleman's bike.

Late one Saturday afternoon, about ten minutes before my class ended, my wife came to the institute. She had had some business to take care of in town and dropped by to visit with the children and the Korean teachers who normally taught the children, and to accompany me on my return to our apartment on campus. Her arrival was greeted with pleasure by one and all, and we stopped class early to have some fun and drink coffee and tea with the owner. We stayed on about half an hour later than usual, and it had become almost dark when we went outside and prepared to leave.

"How are you going to get home?" I asked my wife. "Are you going to run alongside while I ride my bike?"

"I don't know," she answered. "Maybe we could both walk and you could push your bike."

It was a beautiful evening, and we didn't have to hurry. Three or four of the children were gathered around us, wide-eyed and serious. They understood completely the dilemma of having only one bike for two people, and they did not want my wife to walk while I rode.

"Teacher!" one of the girls spoke up. "I know what to do." She patted the rack over the back fender of the bike. "She can ride here."

"Of course, she can," I said. "Why didn't I think of that?" In Korea, it's quite common for older couples (although my wife wasn't old) to ride double on a bicycle. I always thought it looked charming and very cozy.

I agreed immediately and so did my wife. I mounted the bicycle and held it steady while she climbed on. She was wearing jeans but rode side-saddle, with both legs to one side. She put her right arm around my waist, and I pushed off to ride down the street to the edge of town. She waved to the children, who had followed us for several yards, and then we gradually pulled away from the small group and made our way past the few remaining houses.

Once we reached the rice fields, I stopped to lean over the handlebars and tilted the light generator so that the generator wheel would come in contact with the front tire, thus providing us with just enough light for our journey in what was to be a perfect pastoral interlude. That short ride remains one of the most enchanting and romantic moments of my life, and as we continued, she put both arms around my waist and leaned her head against my back, and I slowly pumped her home.

At Home

There are a new table and two new chairs in my apartment. The blond furniture matches perfectly the color of the wooden floor, which is the dominant feature of my Korean abode. The lady of the house keeps the floor absolutely without blemish, and the spotless condition of the entire domicile gives new meaning to the word "clean," even by domestic Korean standards.

The new chairs please me greatly, because now I don't have to sit on the floor. I don't mind sitting of the floor, but my knees and ankles complain rather bitterly when I have to stand up. The table supplies a comfortable place for me to eat and write, and my back is very grateful that my lap no longer serves as a writing desk. Sleeping on the floor has ever bothered me.

In spite of the obvious pragmatic delights of my new acquisitions, aesthetically, they are no more than passing fair. The objects themselves are not beautiful—inexpensive wood with a smooth finish and a strong, rustic design. But their accidental placement before the sliding glass doors that open to the veranda has produced stunning results.

Let me explain. Every morning I awaken before sunrise to study, write, and drink coffee, not always in that order. This morning, after I had written about an hour, I went back inside the bedroom to fetch some needed article for my work, and I had not realized the sun had risen. When I returned, the room had become flooded with very soft, indirect sunlight, and it glowed with impressionistic charm. In remarkable contrast with the shimmering light, the legs of the chairs and table rose straight as arrows from the floor to run parallel with the gray frames of the glass doors and the gray bars of the veranda railing. The bars' shadows cast diagonal gray lines on the veranda floor, and the unlikely mixture of blond and gray produced a subdued vignette that would please the palate of any discerning eye. The strong lines surrounded by undulating early morning light gave the room a Kafkaesque surrealism, yet pleasant and friendly. It was an unexpected surprise to find in an apartment located on dusty Highway 122, just north of Song Jeong Ri.

Shall I awaken my companion and show her my wonderful discovery? No, she will maintain only that the windows are dirty and that the floor needs scrubbing. She will sit in the opposite chair and chide me about my numerous shortcomings. She will not notice that her fair skin matches exactly the color of the new furniture and her sacred floor.

Swimming

The Naktong River is the longest river in South Korea. It rises in the Taebek Mountains and flows just over five hundred kilometers south (with westerly inclinations at times) to Busan, where it empties into the South Sea. In Gumi, the first town I lived in when I came to Korea, the river moves in a leisurely, relaxed tempo and never seems to rush. Throughout its course, at least the parts I've seen, it often has flat, sandy banks that rise almost imperceptibly from the water's edge and, in many places, are forty or fifty meters wide.

One hot summer's day, I declared to my favorite short person that I was going to go swimming.

"Where are you going to go?" she asked suspiciously.

"In the river. I can walk over there in ten minutes."

"That's not a good idea," she declared. "Nobody goes swimming in the river."

"Well, I'm going and you can come, too, if you want." I knew she couldn't swim, but she could watch and give advice.

She got ready and we made the short walk to the river. On our side, the bank was about fifteen feet high and was covered with bushes and some small trees. It was a bit steep, but I was able to scramble down the embankment without too much difficulty. She remained on top.

"That water is dangerous!" she shouted.

"Don't worry, so am I," I said, and slid into the water and swam four or five meters in the gentle current toward the sandy shore on the opposite side.

"That water is dirty!" she shouted again.

"Don't worry, so am I."

She gave up and watched as I swam easily across to the other side. As I knew it would be, the water was much deeper than it looked from the shore or highway bridge. From a distance, it looked as if you could walk to the other side. No way! I swam to the sandy flats that were covered in about four inches of water and managed to get a comfortable resting place on the soft sand about fifteen feet from the flowing water. It was a nice, hot afternoon, and I enjoyed sitting in the sand in the shallow water. I waved to her across the river, and she waved back. It was too far for her to shout at me.

I remained seated for two or three minutes before I realized that I was slowly sinking down into the sand. The sand was watery, very soft and comfortable (too comfortable) and, as she had warned—very dangerous. I worked hard not to panic, and although my heart was beating like a jackhammer, I very slowly rolled over to one side and stretched out, flat on my stomach, so as not to have my entire weight centered on my butt, like moments before. I relaxed my legs and let them trail behind me and then used my arms only, in a breast stroke-type motion, to propel myself over the sand and shallow water the ten feet to the deeper water. It was scary, and my pulse races even now while writing about it. If that wasn't quicksand, then it was close enough for me. No wonder nobody swims in the Naktong River. The water is not dangerous, but the sand will get you.

I was very happy to be in the safety of the river channel and swam back across to the other side. The current had carried me down about fifty meters below where I had entered, and she walked down on top of the bank to meet me as I got out of the water and struggled up through the bushes. She was not happy.

"Look at you!" she said. "Look how wet and dirty you are! Americans are dirty!"

"How many Americans do you know?" I countered.

"One."

Now, there are some discussions you're not going to win, and you might as well take a dive in the first. I pointed to an outdoor table next to a rustic fish-restaurant a little farther along the bank and suggested we go over there and I could dry off in the sun and we could have a Coke. She accepted, and afterwards, when we returned to the house, we got in the shower and she gave me a good scrubbing. Don't ever take a shower with an angry Korean nurse. She'll wash stuff three times you never knew you had in the first place. But that's another story.

Small Town Boys

Some days ago, I left my small apartment without my key and upon my return found the door locked tight. My wife would not be home until late afternoon, and consequently, I spent several hours sitting on a bench in the park in Song Jeong Ri.

It was a splendid day.

There was a light rain, and the beautiful ladies who passed me by with their colorful umbrellas reminded me of Judith Jamison of the Alvin Ailey Dancers. I first saw her in Vienna in 1976, when she appeared alone on stage in a long white dress carrying a white parasol. Her dancing was superb, and the performance of the entire troupe set the standard by which I have measured all other stage performances since.

Alvin Ailey was my neighbor. He was born in Rogers, Texas, a squalid village of some two hundred people located on the Blackland Prairie about ten kilometers from my boyhood home. My father, who was a law officer from Oklahoma, Indian Territory, declared Rogers "the toughest town in Texas," which had rooms reserved twenty-four hours a day at the state penitentiary for many of its fine, upstanding citizens. That a jerkwater town like Rogers could produce a distinguished artist of international stature such as Alvin Ailey is remarkable, indeed. It can happen, but seldom.

Alvin Ailey wasn't the only resident of a small town to achieve international acclaim. Franz Joseph Haydn, the renowned Austrian composer, was born in Rohrau, a small village on the plains of Burgenland close to the Neusiedler Sea. Rohrau is only slightly larger than Rogers but possesses a provincial charm that most inhabitants of Rogers could not comprehend or even dream about. In Rohrau, the thatched roofed farmhouses look exactly the same as the traditional houses one sees in the Korean countryside. The people look the same and view strangers with the same open-mouthed stares that foreigners everywhere encounter when walking through rural areas. But geniuses have got to come from somewhere, and Rohrau's most famous son put the village on the map forever.

For almost thirty years, Haydn was a "salary man" for the Hungarian prince, Nikolaus Esterhazy. He spent his life between Eisenstadt, located just southeast of Vienna and only a few kilometers from his hometown, and Esterhaza, the prince's luxurious palatial estates on the plains of Hungary, and until his patron died, lived and worked in the country. He was not particularly concerned with outside interests and in his words (I translate freely and from memory), "I was cut off from the influences and trials and tribulations of the world, and consequently had to become original."

After the prince died, Haydn moved to Vienna, where great orchestras and an adoring public awaited him. Haydn had already become quite famous, a difficult feat to accomplish in the country, and he was commissioned by England's foremost impresario to write several symphonies for the London Symphony Orchestra. Haydn accepted his offer, wrote twelve wonderful compositions, and since that time symphonic music has not been the same.

And so, when you must spend some unexpected time sitting in the park or taking a walk down by the river just across the way from our campus, enjoy the people you meet. Be nice to them. Who knows what special plans and abilities they may have? Because sometimes, country folk can do well in the big city. Very well.

Ducks and Chicks

Living within a different culture is often fraught with mistakes, misunderstandings, embarrassments, and very funny situations. I have been living in Korea for almost nine years, and every day is an adventure for me. I love getting on the 500 bus and can hardly wait to see what other strange creatures are accompanying me. It's not always comfortable on the 500—or any other city bus, for that matter—but it's always interesting.

A few days ago, I climbed into the bus and immediately felt that this was to be a unique experience. For one thing, I was the youngest aboard. Fortunately, I was in no danger of losing my seat because there were only five or six other old codgers on their way to Song Jeong Ri. I took my seat, relaxed, and was enjoying the passing rice fields and farmhouses when out of the blue, as plain as day, I heard a duck quack. "Quack, quack, quack," it said loudly. I was extremely surprised and grabbed the railing on the seat in front of me with white-knuckled intensity, lunged to my feet, and only barely stifled a shout. "By God! I heard a duck quack!" I remained calm, however, sat back down and, in my best 007 sort of way, looked discreetly about me to see if anyone else had heard the same. I was wearing dark glasses. Perfect for the occasion.

To the best of my considerable powers of observation, no one showed the least sign or interest that we all may have been riding with a feathered, non-paying passenger. I thought perhaps I had been mistaken and attributed the phenomenon to increasing old age and a tendency to be "jumpy" whenever I heard unexpected loud noises, real or imagined.

I had settled back in my seat and was waiting to disembark at the major intersection in Song Jeong Ri when I heard it again. "Quack, quack, quack!" A happy sound, I leaned out and looked up the aisle and just behind the driver's seat was a cardboard box with a hole cut in the side through which protruded a white duck's neck, head and bright yellow bill. "Quack, quack, quack," he chimed again. He was having a very good time, and we old codgers smiled and nodded, amused companions in his temporary good spirits.

When I reached my destination, I stepped out of the bus and realized it was the Five Day Market in Song Jeong Ri, and the duck's owner was carrying him briskly toward the poultry stalls where, without doubt, a grim fate awaited him.

Once, when riding home on the same bus but in a different direction, I was crammed in the aisle, clutching the strap that hangs from the ceiling for those unfortunates who were not able to obtain a place to sit. I was tired and my feet were killing me.

I had noticed a fetching young lady of nineteen or twenty who was sitting close to where I was standing, and I could tell she liked me. She was giving me the eye. She glanced at me with that stunning Korean smile that is wonderfully commonplace here in the Land of the Morning Calm. She got up out of her chair and took a step toward me, and I knew she was going to proposition me and my answer was going to be yes. Hell, yes!

She asked in excellent English, "Would you like to sit down? Please take my seat."

No. Hell, no!

I was very disappointed, but I think I concealed my chagrin in an admirable fashion and, after only a moment's hesitation, accepted her offer and sat down. She smiled sweetly and grabbed on to the ceiling strap with practiced competence that assured me she could ride standing up better than I.

I hail from Texas, where the men never sit while ladies stand. Even after almost nine years of immersion in Korean culture and tradition, I'm still a little bit embarrassed and uncomfortable to sit in a chair while ladies around me are standing. But I'm getting used to it.

Japanese Girls

When I first moved to Korea, I lived in Gumi. By Korean standards, it's a small city, about 330,000 people, located twenty-five miles northwest of Daegu. I had a job teaching English at an institute there and had students ranging in age from seven or eight years old to folks almost as old as I was.

One Saturday, some of my older men students suggested we take a hike up Gumo Mountain and have a drink and an afternoon snack at one of the many watering holes, shops, and restaurants located along the way. Mountain hiking is a very popular pastime in Korea, and the trails and paths are often quite crowded on the weekends. My students were all businessmen in their mid-thirties or so, and I accepted their suggestion, as long as they wouldn't take their hiking more seriously than the eating and drinking. They laughed and said that they planned to be hiking about thirty minutes throughout the entire afternoon and that would be the extent of it.

We met at the city park at the base of the main trail and started our climb. They were dressed casually, with the ubiquitous red vest and various other required paraphernalia, and I was wearing my brown, flat-crowned Bradford cowboy hat, which was guaranteed to get astonished looks from just about everybody. It was the handsomest hat I've ever owned. We went slowly, with frequent stops to admire the view, and we stopped off at one of those snack stands to have a beer and some dried squid—not an attractive combination, in my opinion. After that, we stopped again at a particularly pleasant spot to enjoy the warm sunshine and catch our breath.

There were two young ladies there who took a very charming interest in me and my hat, probably not in that order. They were perhaps twenty-one or twenty-two years old but looked to be fifteen or so to my, as yet, unaccustomed western eye. They laughed and smiled at me and waved me over to join them. They wanted one of my companions to take a photo with the three of us (four, counting my hat), and they each asked to wear my hat for a picture. They entwined their arms in mine, leaned their heads on my shoulder, put their arms around me, and flirted very unselfconsciously while my friends took photos with the girls' cameras.

We finished the shoot and parted most cordially, saying our goodbyes with many smiles and waves.

After we left and began our descent off the mountain, I said, "By God, I've been in Korea for six months, and since that time not one Korean woman has touched me or shown any kind of physical attraction toward me in any way. Man, I had a good time!"

My companions laughed and one said, "Well, Mr. Jack, there's a reason for that."

"Yeah? What is it?"

"They're Japanese!" he said, and they all laughed.

I stayed almost one year in Gumi and then moved to Gwang ju to teach English at Honam University. The university was situated on a rural campus southwest of the city, and after three years there, my wife and I moved to the top floor of the new dormitory for international women students. We had a beautiful large apartment with a wonderful view of the river and rice fields, which were just across the main, and only, road to the campus. It was a perfect place for this Texas country boy.

At the dorm, most of the time, I would ride in the elevator that was often packed with beautiful young ladies, all with black hair, all, by western standards, relatively short, and all saturating the small, enclosed space with the most refreshing smell of early morning soap and water. I was once crowded into the corner of the elevator with my late friend, Michel, in the opposite corner, and our eyes met as we looked across the sea of black hair and smiling eyes, and he commented, "And we get paid for this!"

Early one evening, I entered the elevator on the bottom floor and realized that the interior lights were out, and after the door closed, it was black as the pits of hell in there. No problem. I like the dark. The elevator stopped at the next floor, the door opened automatically, and in stepped one of our Japanese students to ride to the fifth floor. I knew her by sight, and that she was Japanese, but we were nodding acquaintances only, although she was always very friendly and polite. I was watching her as the door stated to close and observed the panicked look in her face and eyes as she realized there was no light in the elevator and that she would be riding in the elevator with me in the dark. Alone. I thought she was going to jump out at the last second, but I watched her gather her courage and determination to ride the distance.

I didn't move a muscle, one way or the other, but after the door closed and we were on our way, I spoke to her. "Now, don't try to kiss me while we're here in the dark."

She burst out laughing and continued to giggle until we reached her fifth-floor stop—a very short journey, she told me later. After that, we became very friendly acquaintances and enjoyed on-campus coffee together from time to time. A bold, brave, and no-nonsense young lady, she was. Japanese style.

In Korea, it is sometimes necessary for foreign workers to leave the country to obtain some required information or fill out some required papers in order to be granted our working visas. My favorite foreign destination for such matters is Fukuoka, a port city in Japan, located pretty much due east of Busan, the most important port on Korea's east coast. I always travel to Fukuoka by a fast hydroplane ferry that travels at some sixty knots an hour and covers the distance in about three hours.

Fukuoka is a wonderful city of about 1.5 million and is very clean, quiet, and civilized. Everything works, people read newspapers on the subway, cars cannot honk their horns, the food's excellent, children are polite and very cute, everyone is friendly, and the Korean consulate is efficient.

On my last trip to Fukuoka, I had completed all my business by 10:30 A.M., and I got back to the port in time to catch the 2:00 P.M. ferry back to Busan. I got my ticket and boarded the ferry at the proper time and took an unreserved seat in the middle of the third or fourth row on the lower deck. The seat on my left was vacant until a very attractive woman in her mid-thirties (okay, she was probably forty) came down the aisle and looked the situation over and sat down next to me. Maybe she knew I was a good swimmer and might come in handy. There were several other places she could have chosen, but she chose the one next to me. Always a good sign. She gave me a short smile and sat down.

The boat eased off the dock and quickly set out to sea. We hadn't been traveling fifteen minutes when her head began to nod, and I risked a quick glance to confirm that her eyes were closed. She kept leaning, closer and closer until her head was resting very comfortably on my shoulder. At least I was very comfortable. After a few minutes, all of a sudden, she jerked awake, raised her head, and sat back up. I don't remember if I smiled at her or not, but ten minutes later she was again sleeping on my shoulder and had slipped her right arm inside my arm, and there she remained for the rest of the journey.

About three minutes before we docked, she sat up and smiled at me.

"Thank you," she said. "I was very tired and trusted you. You have a nice face."

I wanted to comment on some of the nice things she had but could only manage, "Will you be staying long in Korea?"

"Two weeks," she answered. "At my sister's house. She has lived in Korea for many years. Her husband will be picking me up at the dock."

And with that, and without a backward glance, she walked out of the ferry, down the gangway, and disappeared into the crowd.

Indonesian Girls

In my Gumi neighborhood, there were several factories, and many of them hired foreign workers to do the grunt work. The grunt workers made less money than Korean workers but more than they could make in their home countries. I suspect it was not an ideal set-up for the foreigners, but using workers from poorer countries to do the dirty work in more affluent countries is not unique to Korea. It's a worldwide phenomenon.

When walking around close to my house, I often met a group of young girls who were always on their way to or from work at one of the nearby factories. There were about ten of them, two of whom were a bit older, perhaps in their late twenties, who watched over the younger ones. Reminded me of the nanny-goats watching the flocks of fluffy white kids on the flat mountaintops of Bosque County. Exactly like that. The ladies were from Indonesia and were always very friendly and cheerful, and it was very pleasant to meet them on the street.

One afternoon at about 2:00, I was writing at my desk and I heard a knock at my apartment door. I got up, walked over, and opened it wide. All the Indonesian girls were congregated there on the narrow stairway landing, and one of the older girls asked, "Hi, Jack, may we come in?"

I was very pleasantly surprised but recovered quickly. "Of course, please do come in." I had no idea they knew where I lived. "I am honored to have so many beautiful young ladies at my home at one time. Please sit down."

They all sat down on the floor in the living room. I don't remember that I had any chairs at all in that apartment, except in the kitchen.

Before I could say anything more, one of the nannies asked, "Could we sleep here for two hours?"

"Of course. Make yourselves at home."

And they did just that. They all lay down on the floor, using sweaters and jackets and each other for pillows, and the lot of them were asleep within two minutes.

I continued my writing and worked on as if they weren't there. A couple of times I glanced all around the room, and I must say that I've never seen so many curves on one floor in all my life.

By the clock, the two shepherds awoke after two hours and roused the girls from their slumbers. They all got up, gathered their things, and trooped out my door.

"Thank you, Jack." They smiled and bowed to me as they left.

They never offered any explanation concerning their strange request for two hours' hospitality on my living room floor, and I never asked. Good neighbors don't always need explanations.

Korean Wives and Money

In Korea, the women keep the money and manage all financial affairs for the family. It took about five years for this Texas country boy to come to grips with this fact and acquiesce to the mores and customs of this aspect of Korean culture. If my hometown buddies knew that I meekly turn over all my wages to my cute little wife, they'd never speak to me again. "Hell, that's crazy!" they'd say. "It's unpatriotic!—It's vegetarian!"

After fifteen years of having no money close to hand, I've come to rather enjoy it. Life is a lot simpler. I can look panhandlers in the eye and tell them with convincing sincerity that I'm just as broke as they are. I drink machine coffee for fifteen cents a cup. It's tasty! I ride my bike a lot. It's healthy and a lot of fun. (It's also just a little bit dangerous.) My wife does give me a meager weekly allowance, the sum of which would embarrass the poorest middle school student in town, but it's okay.

We sometimes go out with friends to traditional Korean restaurants, where we take off our shoes and sit on the floor. (I hate sitting on the floor, but that's a story for another day.) After sitting on the floor for an hour or more, I have difficulty getting up and putting my knees and ankles in working order, finding my shoes, putting them on, and making it to the cashier to pay my fair share. When Koreans are finished eating, they get up immediately and leave the table. They almost never relax and talk over a slow cup of tea or coffee after a meal. They put their chopsticks down after the last bite, stand up, put their shoes on, and pay the bill before I'm able to get my old legs out from underneath the low, sit-on-the-floor table. Then, I get nervous and choke under the pressure of trying to find my shoes and put them on without falling down or bumping into something. By the time I get my shoes on, the Koreans have paid the bill and are already outside in the parking lot, smoking a cigarette.

When my wife is along, it's no problem at all. She goes to pay the bill while I crawl around looking for my shoes, and I am able to take my own good time about it all.

During the first year or so of my futile fight for my natural-born right to control the money I earned by the sweat of my brow, I asked my wife why we shouldn't agree to sixty-forty deal about the money business. She could have 60 percent and I'd take 40 percent. That sounded like a fair proposition to me.

"No way," she said. "I'm keeping all of it."

"But that's not right!" I protested. "Hell, I earn it."

"Nope."

"Why not?"

"Men don't need to have any money. If men have money, they just spend it on women and alcohol."

What was I supposed to say to that? It was the beginning of the end.

"I keep all the money and save it for the later," she declared. And she did, and she does.

When I first came to Korea, I was paid my salary in cash. The boss put the money in a white envelope and gave it to me every two weeks, or at the end of the month. It was great. All everyday working folks were paid like that. But electronic banking has ruined the lives of most married men in Korea. Now we never even see the cash. There are just numbers in a bank book that won't buy anything unless you've got a couple of plastic cards and a bunch of secret numbers memorized.

But we guys in Korea have got some good company. I read just the other day that Prince Charles never carries any money on his person. Hey, just like me! If he can go all the places he goes, do all the things he does, and wear all those beautiful clothes he's got with not one penny in his pocket, then that makes me feel a lot better. If it's good enough for Prince Chuck, it's good enough for me.

Is his wife Korean?

Korean Education

In my opinion, Korean school children are, for the most part, abused by their world-renowned education system, in conjunction with and abetted by their parents. On school days, you will see uniformed children on the city bus at 6:30 a.m., and if for some perverted, unfortunate reason you happen to be on the bus at 10:30 or 11:00 p.m., you will see the same students, in the same uniforms, but traveling in a different direction—home, I would hope. It's not right. For students who are nineteen or twenty years old, spending sixteen hours a day getting an education is fine if they want to. For middle school and high school students who are forced to by their parents and the ever-present scholastic competition in this country, I think that's too much.

In addition, when I first came to Korea fifteen years ago, the students attended classes on Saturdays as well. Nevertheless, I must give credit where credit is due, and some enlightened parents and lawmakers have managed to change that draconian custom to only one Saturday every two weeks at the present time. That's progress. Unfortunately, I regret to report that on those two holiday Saturdays per month, most students attend special institutes to brush up their skills that might possibly get rusty over a two-day weekend.

When do they get to have any fun? They don't have time to learn how to swim or play baseball. How educated are you, really, when you don't know how to swim or play baseball? Are Korean students better educated or smarter than American or Austrian students? They are not. American and Austrian students do not go to school on weekends. They enjoy themselves for a day or two, and I think that makes them better students, come Monday morning.

My late friend and colleague, Frank Callaghan, had a school-aged daughter who attended Korean public school in Song Jeong Ri, a small town close to our university workplace, not far from Gwang-ju City. He informed the school authorities that his daughter, Maria, would not be attending school on Saturdays because she would be playing football (soccer) with university faculty and friends. Her grades did not suffer, and she played outside on Saturdays and got some practical education that one simply cannot obtain in a school classroom. Korean parents need that kind of courage and sound thinking. Of course, Frank accompanied his daughter on her weekend activities.

He didn't send her—he took her.

In my university classes, I ask my students if they want their children to be able to relax and have fun on the weekends, or go to school and study like they did. They agree unanimously that going to school on Saturdays is a bad idea.

"Then fix it," I tell them. And you know what? I think they will.

I remain optimistic about the educational system in Korea. There are some teachers who agree with my assessment that the students work too long and too hard and are not treated in kind and reasonable manner. I know they're out there.

*   *   *

Some years ago, I taught at an English institute and had an early morning class at 6:30. It was in the deep mid-winter, and I was waiting on the sidewalk at the next-to-the-last bus stop in the small town, which provided my introduction to life in Korea. The time was 6:00 A.M., and it was pitch dark and damned cold. The deserted street was not well lit and the overall ambience was, in a word, grim.

I was on my way to teach a class to a group of young businessmen downtown who had regular jobs during the daylight hours but wanted to improve their English skills and were serious enough to meet at 6:30 to accomplish their goals. I have always been an early riser, they were nice fellows, and I enjoyed the class, the uncivilized hour notwithstanding.

As I was waiting, I was joined by a young girl of about sixteen. She did not speak to me or even acknowledge my presence, and I did her the favor of not being too friendly, as is my wont, and left her alone. It was not a cheery place or time, and foreigners of my ilk can be dangerous, and there was not a single soul in evidence who might come to her aid if she were to find herself in a difficult situation. She was wearing the ubiquitous school uniform, and I guess she was getting an early start on her school-day activities.

We continued waiting for several minutes, and she suddenly walked away from me and the bus stop to the entrance of a small store about forty feet distant. There was a weak, depressing light coming from a bulb hanging naked above the entranceway. She sat down on the top step about a yard off the sidewalk and swung her school backpack to her lap and started fumbling with the straps to open it.

By God, I thought. *She's going to take out a book and study while she's waiting for the bus in these shit surroundings. I'm impressed.*

I watched, but carefully so as not to alarm her, and I saw her reach into her backpack and pull out...a large white pillow! I was very surprised that it wasn't a book of some kind, but its size must have taken up all the space in her backpack. No room for books. She put the pillow on her knees and laid her head on top in order to catch a few moments of shut-eye while she waited for the bus.

It was very cute and it made me smile. I'm still smiling. Perhaps the Korean education system is not so pushy and demanding as its reputation would have us believe. This young lady obviously had a teacher somewhere along the way of her daily routine who would allow her to bring a pillow to school and use it. Somebody has got his/her priorities straight. There may be hope for the Korean school system yet.

Two days before typing the final draft of this short commentary, the powers-that-be in Korea have declared, starting next year, that there will be no more public school classes on Saturdays, period. My optimism is not unfounded.

In Memoriam

April 4 marks the first anniversary of the tragic death of my good friend and colleague, Frank Callaghan. For those of you who never knew him, he was a distinguished teacher here at Yeungnam University, a very fine writer and editor, draftsman, self-taught musician, humorist, and devoted husband and father. I still can't believe he's gone.

The advent of spring on our campus is breathtakingly beautiful, and nobody ever appreciated it more than Frank. He was one of the very few men I have known who was in the habit of buying flowers for himself and placing them on his desk for his own pleasure and the enjoyment of anybody else who might happen by. Despite the fact that he was one of the rough, tough lads from Liverpool, he had a keen aesthetic sense.

On that day, I wrote in my diary, "Today is about the most perfect day one can imagine. The cherry trees on campus are splendid. The weather is clear and sunny and…it could not be more beautiful." And on that day, he mounted his powerful BMW and rode slowly up the cherry-lined hill just southwest of the FLI, to keep his final date with destiny.

Who could have known? Frank the Invincible, we sometimes called him.

I miss the Sunday morning coffees at his house, his quoting of *Hamlet* on the veranda at La Cantina, his wonderful, unique advice when I asked for it, our playing football with his daughter on Saturdays when she was supposed to be in school, and the quiet times when no words were necessary. A good friend he was—and still is.

In a day or two, I will leave the FLI and walk down past the Mirror Pond and up the same cherry-blossomed road to meet my good friend, Frank. I know he will be waiting for me. We'll greet each other warmly, and I'll clap him enthusiastically on the back as we continue our short journey up the hill. We'll talk of battles won and lost, the many songs we have sung, the good old days, and the way it used to be in spring.

A Korean Christmas Story

There is a small farm village located up in the mountains about an hour's drive due north of the Daegu Opera House. It's just a loose collection of houses, really, maybe ten or fifteen altogether, not substantial or important enough to be called a proper village. Despite its relative proximity to a very large city, the hamlet is painfully rustic, quiet, and very lonely. I have visited the area on several occasions and have been struck by two things in particular: the complete darkness after sundown and the bone-deep cold that starts early in the winter and seems to last forever. Unless my memory fails me, I've never visited there except in winter, and I can imagine, only with difficulty, the warm and sunny days that surely must accompany the late spring and summer seasons.

My parents-in-law used to live in the village in a small four-room house located on the southern edge of the cluster of houses. After Dad's passing, Mom stayed on for three or four more years, spending the coldest months with us down in the city, but maintaining her residence and independence at the mountain house most of the time. Just over three years ago, she gave in (not up) and grudgingly agreed to live with us on a fulltime basis. Her presence has enriched our lives, and I think she is happy to be with us, although I've never drummed up the courage to ask her. She's too old to be living at the mountain house by herself, and she's better off living with us. She knows it and we know it, and that's all there is to it. We've never needed to discuss it.

Late one evening, a few days before last Christmas, Mom called my wife into her room and whispered to her confidentially that she had just remembered hiding a goodly amount of money behind her bedroom dresser at the mountain house. Needless to say, my wife was surprised and asked her mother why she had waited so long to tell her such a thing.

"I just remembered it in my dream," she explained.

Okay.

During the course of the following two or three days, she described in detail the exact location of the hiding place, the color of the wallet she used, and the amount, about 350,000 won, she had deposited therein. On the strength of her convictions, we decided to undertake an expedition to the mountain house, which had stood abandoned and desolate for over two years, and search for the hidden treasure.

On the next Saturday, after finally completing our weekend chores, at the late hour of 10:00 P.M., we loaded our gear into the little gray car and left for the mountain house. Our gear consisted of one powerful flashlight, gloves, and a sack of fresh oranges, just in case. I wished for a loaded pistol or at least a gleaming cutlass that would flash in the moonlight, but those faithful companions in my days of yore had long-since forsaken me for more adventuresome cohorts with worthier pursuits. There wasn't any moonlight that night anyway.

On the way, we stopped off in Daegu to pick up my wife's sister, and the three of us proceeded to our mountain destination. We successfully navigated the winding, narrow roads, which became increasingly steep and difficult as we approached the point of our treasure rendezvous, and at midnight exactly, we pulled up in what passed for a driveway and climbed out of the car. There was not a light to be seen anywhere, the skies were crystal clear, and it was cold and silent. In places where the sun could not reach, the ground was covered in snow and the barren spots reached by the afternoon sun were ankle-deep in frozen mud and slush.

The nearest neighbor's house was about a hundred meters to the north, and as we struggled and stumbled around the wall to the rear of the house, I felt uncomfortable sneaking around in complete darkness, as quietly as possible in the middle of the night, trying not to be noticed or discovered while on a probable fool's errand searching for hidden treasure. But I must admit, it was exciting.

We gained entrance to the house through the unlocked front door and turned right, through the living room and into the bedroom. The chifforobe and dresser were standing on the left wall, just as Mom had described. We pulled out the dresser and looked behind where the wallpaper and floor linoleum met and they were loose, having become unglued, just as Mom had described. I held the light while my wife and her sister ripped off the wallpaper and pulled up the linoleum to find exactly nothing. We moved the large chifforobe and scrambled behind it in the opposite corner. Nothing. I tilted the chifforobe and the ladies looked underneath with the same results. We took out every drawer, examined all the contents of each one and, after an hour or so, declared our trip a failure. It was a small room and the three of us had searched enough. There was no hidden wallet with 350,000 won inside.

We looked at each other and laughed a bit, and to tell the truth, I was not overly disappointed. I had had a great time. I never really expected to find anything of value anyway, and I had not broken my neck sneaking around the back of the house through recalcitrant vine entanglements and snow-filled ditches, and nobody had called the cops—a pretty successful evening by my standards. At 1:00 A.M. we climbed back into the car and I cranked the engine.

From the back seat, the ladies passed me a delicious orange, already peeled, and we headed back to the bright lights of the big city.

After about twenty minutes, we reached the major highway and I noticed in my rearview mirror the ladies smiling and giggling in the back seat. It just occurred to me that my wife never rides in the back seat when I'm driving. What was she doing back there having such a good time?

At my inquiry, she answered, "We're counting up the money!"

"What money?" I asked. "Did you find the wallet when I wasn't looking?"

"Of course not," she answered. "It's the money we brought with us."

I didn't understand.

"We didn't really believe we'd find anything, so we brought 350,000 won in old bills to give to Mom when we get back. So she won't be disappointed."

As politely as I could, I suggested that Mom was old enough to be told the truth, and that we had made this trip for nothing, and the 350 thou they were counting so gleefully probably belonged to me. (I didn't actually say that last part, but I thought it, for sure.) Unfortunately, their minds were already made up and they refused to take my opinion seriously about the matter, and they generously offered me another orange in consolation.

I kept my mouth shut during the rest of the trip, and we dropped off my wife's sister at her apartment near the Opera House and eventually arrived at our own place in Gyeongsan at 3:00 A.M. I went in and went straight to bed and my wife told Mom, who was in bed but wide awake, that we had had a very successful trip and had found the money exactly where she said it was. Mom was ecstatic, and it was only with some difficulty and promises to count the money in the morning that my wife was able to convince Mom to stay in bed and go back to sleep.

I awoke at sunup that morning and sat in the kitchen with a cup of coffee and planned my schedule for the day. Mom marched in after a few minutes with a huge grin on her face, and I knew instantly that her two daughters had done the right thing. When my wife joined us, she explained that Mom wanted to give her grandchildren some cash and that she would take all of us out to eat in the very near future. After that, with all the money left over, she wanted to finance a trip to Yeongdeok, on the East Sea, and eat crabs.

Well, she was as good as her word and spread that money around as if she'd just won the lottery. Her joy at being able to be generous to her family was as fine a Christmas gift as I ever hope to see. Had we not searched for the hidden treasure and, by hook and crook, returned with the booty, I would have missed it. To the best of my knowledge, she gave all of it away and kept not one farthing for herself.

A couple of days later, I noticed a 10,000 won note lying on the breakfast table in the kitchen.

"Mom," I called out. "Is this your money?"

She came into the room and, with a sweet smile, picked up the bill and put it in my shirt pocket.

My wife translated. "Mom wants to give you this for driving all the way to her house this past weekend and bringing home the money she had hidden."

"I was glad to do it," I declared. "It was a trip I'll never forget." And I won't.

Besides, the ten bucks she gave me was ten bucks more than I would have ever seen if those two Korean sisters in the back seat had been passing out my money.

What goes around comes around, and sometimes things work out just right.

Merry Christmas!

Attack Chili!

B ack home in Indiana, my Texas-born wife prided herself on making the
finest chili to be found anywhere north of the Red River. She spent most
of her time playing the piano, but when she took time off to move from the
piano bench to the kitchen to cook chili—well, she did it right.

One Sunday evening, we invited our good friends, Bill and Candy, over
to our place for a chili supper. They were excited about coming to our house,
because all week I'd been telling them what great chili my wife made and she'd
worked hard to live up to the enthusiastic billing I'd given her.

The evening went extremely well, and we all had a wonderful time. There
was plenty of chili, chips, and salsa, and we ate a lot and quaffed generous
amounts of Stroh's Beer to wash it all down. Bill and Candy left at a reasonable
hour because the next day was Monday and we had rigorous schedules of study
and teaching at the Music School. We accompanied them to their car and
wished them good night as they drove off, and then we went back inside and
cleaned up the kitchen. The evening had been a big success.

Early Monday morning, around 4:30, I was awakened by the faint, telltale
signs of an impending attack of Santa Anna's revenge, which is not uncommon
after a serious evening of Tex-Mex fare, even the finest. I rolled out of bed and
was slowly making my way to the toilet, when my bowels were hit by a short,
painful spasm that would have made a Spartan sob. I leapt for the bathroom
door and managed to get inside and seated on the stool, just in the nick of
time. Surely, I need not describe here the events of the next five minutes or so,
but suffice it to say that my mission was successfully performed, and
afterwards, I stood up and went to the washbasin to splash cold water on my
face and sooth my fevered brow. I washed up and returned to bed and lay
down next to the cook and had every intention of going back to sleep for
another hour. After about ten minutes, I was forced to make a return trip to
the bathroom for a repeat performance, and I'm sorry to report that in the
ensuing sixty minutes, I did several encores, which were not demanded by an
adoring audience but by dire necessity.

I had to be at school early that day, and my wife got my clothes and school paraphernalia ready, and just before 6:00, immediately after my fourth or fifth encore, I quickly put on my clothes, grabbed my things, and ran for the car. It was a fifteen-minute trip to school, and because of the early hour, I figured to get a parking place close to the building and hoped to make it to the nearest men's room in the first basement before the next attack. There was little traffic at that hour, and I made it in record time. I got an excellent parking space and sprinted for the men's room. I ran through the outside door, down the short flight of stairs to the basement, and down the hall. I smashed through the restroom door and skidded to a stop in front of the first stall. I dropped my books on the floor, unbuckled my pants, and sat down. Whew! Made it!

After a couple of minutes, my heavy breathing had subsided and I had ceased to grunt, groan an' what-all, and I slowly became aware that I was not alone in that room. Someone was moving around in the stall next to mine, and I detected some of those familiar restroom sounds that were definitely not my own. I leaned way over to the front and looked to the right, underneath the stall wall panel that, for some reason, is always positioned about a foot and a half off the floor, and saw the left shoe and ankle of my temporary neighbor. The shoe was a very shiny, very expensive, light brown patent leather loafer, accompanied by dark brown socks that matched perfectly.

"Bill, is that you?" I asked cautiously. I was pretty sure I knew who it was, but you want to be careful in such delicate situations and locations.

"It certainly is!" he replied. "How'd you guess? For the last hour and a half of this fine morning, I've been on one toilet or another all over this side of town!" His voice sounded strained and necky, not at all proper for a singer of his caliber. He also spoke with poorly concealed sarcasm and disgust.

"Me, too. It's been a rough morning, and it's not over yet."

"What did your wife put in that chili, anyway? Gunpowder?"

"I don't know, but she must have done something wrong. I made it very clear that neither I nor anybody I know will ever eat her chili again. She felt very remorseful when she wasn't laughing."

"If I don't get better soon, I may call my lawyer!"

"Don't blame you. You've got a good case."

Bill was still there when I left and went to the appointments I had that morning. Around 9:45, I again felt the call and had to make a mad dash to the men's room, but on the third floor this time. I successfully arrived and was more or less comfortably seated when I could not resist the urge to lean forward again and peer under the right wall panel. Sure enough, the shoe was there, still shiny and not scuffed or smudged in any way by the morning's activities, and Bill's leg was still attached.

"How's it going, Bill?"

"Terrific!" he replied. "But Jack, we've got to quit meeting like this. People are starting to talk."

"I know they are, and not without good reason. I've run over a few people in the halls and pushed others rudely aside in my haste to reach the men's room on several floors. I've apologized on the run, and I think they understand."

"Well, I sure do!" he said, and that brought our pre-noon meetings to an end. But I did run into him one more time, later in that afternoon.

Now, in those days at the Indiana School of Music in Bloomington, we had a wonderful fellow in the undergraduate program who was studying piano. He happened to be blind and had a large German Shepherd as his seeing-eye dog. I never learned his name, but he and I had visited on several occasions and we got along just fine. I left his seeing-eye dog alone, which I think you're supposed to do. He, the dog, was friendly enough, but tended to business and did not invite casual familiarity. On that particular afternoon, the dog became sick, perhaps he too had been eating chili, but anyway, the dog could not make it outside in time to relieve himself (and believe you me, I understood his situation completely) and stopped very close to the second-floor lounge and took a huge shit right in front of Tibor Kozma's office door. It was a big pile and it stank with a vengeance, and the smell permeated the entire second floor and even into the open stairways, up and down. It must have been just moments after the incident when I made my way down the same hall and, in my finest Central Texas style (honed to perfection by eighteen years of shoveling shit in the barn), deftly dodged the imposing pile, and joined my friends in the lounge. The students there were having a great time, despite the stench, because Mr. Kozma was not the best-liked man on campus, due to his sharp tongue and uncompromising musical standards, and the general consensus was that the dog could not have picked a better spot.

Later on that afternoon, I gathered my gear and made my way to the exit to get in my car and drive home. As I passed by the men's room in the basement, the door opened and Bill came out with a relaxed and comfortable smile on his face—until he saw me.

"Hey, Bill. You must be doing better."

He wasn't listening and his face turned solemn as he put his hand on my shoulder.

"Jack, man," he spoke as if we were in a funeral home, "I was sure sorry to see that you didn't make it earlier today. It could just as easily have been me. God, that must have been awful!" He wanted to laugh, but the situation was too serious.

"What are you talking about?" I demanded.

"That pile of shit in front of Mr. Kozma's door on the second floor. Did anybody see you?"

"Hell, no! Because I didn't do it! It was that seeing-eye dog. He must have been sick or something."

"No kidding! Well, thank God! And I have been really concerned about you all afternoon. I'm sure glad to find out it wasn't you. Actually, I knew something just didn't add up. It didn't really have that chili smell and the consistency was just too solid. At least compared to the shit I've been sending down the pipes."

This was obviously an eye-witness report. He must have walked by, too. "Jesus," I said. "I didn't know you were such an expert."

"I wasn't until early this morning," he said. "But after eating your wife's chili, I feel I may have the knowledge and experience necessary to make a significant, perhaps crucial, contribution in the field. Maybe I should change my major," he said, as he wandered off toward the stairway that led to the second-floor lounge.

Author's note: Bill did not change his major. He had a very successful singing career in Europe and was the leading tenor at the Zuerich Opera for several years. He is now Dean of the College of Visual and Performing Arts at George Mason University, and he is a distinguished expert in the field of Arts Education.

The Lord's Work

In late August of 1980, I entered the library at the University of Northern Iowa and came out in the following July with a masters degree in music. Getting a masters degree is one of the few really smart things I've done in my life, and at the tender age of thirty-six, with ten years of professional singing under my belt, I finally got a piece of paper to confirm my education.

While working on my degree, I had an assistantship in the music school, teaching voice, and I also received the GI Bill. In addition, I was the music director of an Episcopal Church in Cedar Falls, where I conducted the choir and sang an occasional solo. Consequently, I made enough money for my wife, baby daughter, and me to squeak by.

Now, in those days, the State of Iowa had a draconian law that forbade the selling of alcohol of any kind on Sundays. Why anyone would suggest or support such a law is beyond me, and I can say that I certainly was not responsible for its passing because I was not a legal resident of the State of Iowa and could not vote, one way or the other, so don't blame me.

One Sunday, the three of us were returning from church, and my wife mentioned to me with no small degree of satisfaction that there was not one beer in the house and alcohol could not be purchased on the Lord's Day.

"What are you going to do?" she asked. "All afternoon and evening with no beer. How will you cope?"

"I am not concerned," I answered calmly. "The Lord will provide."

"What?" She raised her voice. "Do you think the Lord is going to provide you with beer today? Incredible! How could you even suggest such a thing?"

"I spend quite a bit of time and energy doing the Lord's work at church. I go every Sunday and have choir rehearsal every Wednesday night. I never miss. I'm never late. I perform my duties at church in a very responsible and, if I may say so, Christian-like manner."

"But that's your job," she persisted. "If they didn't pay you money, you wouldn't go."

"That's true," I said, "but before I got big enough to beat up my mother, I went to church three times a week for seventeen years and nobody ever gave me a nickel. I figure I'm ahead of the game, or behind, depending on how you look at it, but I'm not worried, because if the Lord is keeping track of such things, he'll see that I'm deserving."

"Incredible!" she said again.

"Perhaps not so incredible as you may think. Actually, Jesus' first recorded miracle was changing water into wine. Good wine. It was at that wedding. Don't you remember?" (It's my second-favorite Bible story.)

She said nothing. What could she say? I had the facts down pat. I didn't go to church for seventeen years for totally nothing. I did learn a few things.

It was only a short drive from the church to our place, and I parked my Ford 150 and we all got out. We went in through the main door and walked down the stairs to our basement apartment, and lo and behold! Placed in front of our door, in all its radiant splendor, was an entire case of Rhinelander's best! My wife was speechless. I remained calm and didn't even say I told you so. That would have been tacky.

"Incredible!" she finally managed to sputter for the third time.

"Trust in the Lord, oh ye of little faith," I said as I picked up the case of beer and moved it into the house. "The Lord does indeed work in mysterious ways!"

Author's note: Some months before, with my handy pickup truck, I helped Keith Johnson, professor of trumpet at the University of Northern Iowa, move his family and all their belongings from one apartment to another. He was very grateful and after I refused to accept any payment for my services, he declared he would send me a case of beer. I said fine and promptly forgot about it. On that particular Sunday, he made good on his promise. Hallelujah!

Istanbul

If memory serves me right, I have spent two nights in Istanbul, a fabulous city that surely deserves a few more overnight stays. On both occasions, I was traveling through, on my way to Vienna or Beirut, and due to poor flight connections, it was necessary for me to spend a night.

On the first trip, I arrived at the airport around 9:00 P.M. and my flight out was to leave around 8:00 the next morning. To save money and a lot of hassle, I decided to remain in the airport and catch a little sleep from time to time and just tough it out. I'd done it many times, all over half the world, and once more wasn't going to be a problem. This was in the late 1970s, and at that time, the Istanbul International Airport reminded me of a very large, filthy pigsty. As I walked into the main lobby and waiting area, there was not one place to sit down and it was packed with people, mostly men in white T-shirts and smoking cigarettes. I went outside where the air was a bit fresher, and there were men asleep on the ground, between the hedges and the walls of the building, and (I don't think I'm making this up) in the trees—all of them wearing white T-shirts, and those who were awake, smoking. It was surreal.

I went back inside and looked in vain for a place to sit. In the far corner of the waiting room, there was a bar and I went back there and bought a can of beer. From what I could tell, only in that corner, the smell of cigarette smoke was reduced and replaced by the smell of spilled beer and urine. It was a foul place, and there were a lot of tough-looking guys hanging around that did not add to its overall charm.

I took my beer and went back out into the waiting room and drank it standing up. As there was no place to sit, I found one of the few remaining vacant spots on the wall and leaned into it in the most comfortable angle I could manage and closed my eyes. I had a suitcase with me and put it between my legs and the wall, knowing that if someone wanted to steal it, they'd probably wake me up in the process. I wasn't sure I could go to sleep anyway, just doze from time to time.

Along around 2:00 A.M., I was brought to my senses by a great deal of movement in the large room, and about half the people were getting up and gathering their children and belongings to board a flight out. Without appearing too greedy or self-centered, I managed to get a place to sit in one of the cheap plastic chairs, placed my suitcase directly in front of it, draped my legs over the suitcase, and promptly went to sleep. It was the most comfortable plastic chair I've ever sat in.

After an hour and a half, I awoke to see a pretty young woman standing right in front of me. She was very pregnant, holding a toddler in her right arm, and was riding herd on one or two more troublesome children who were running around in the close vicinity. She looked exhausted. As tired as I was, my Texas upbringing forced me to stand up, sweep off my hat, and offer the only chair within forty miles of the place to her. She didn't move a muscle, but out of the corner of my eye, I saw a movement in my direction and before I knew what was happening, her sorry-assed husband slipped into my vacant chair before you could say Jack Robinson. Son-of-a-bitch! I was astounded and speechless. I looked at her to catch her reaction, and she was looking at him with absolutely no expression on her face whatsoever. She was probably so happy that her husband had a place to sit. Maybe. I wanted to choke him, but discretion is the better part of valor, and I did nothing. Had I thrown him out of the chair, I would have been accosted by fifty or sixty Turks and there was no way I could have whipped 'em all. And so, I picked up my suitcase and went back to my previous spot on the wall. "When in Rome, do as the Romans do." Hell, thirty years later, and I'm still mad about it.

The other time I stopped in Istanbul, it was mid-afternoon, and this time, I had a hotel reservation. I was learning. I had the name of my hotel, which I have long since forgotten, but I checked with information booth folks and asked them about how best to get there.

"Go out the main door and take a taxi," he advised. "And the price is one hundred fifty lira. No more," he added.

I went out the main entrance and was immediately confronted by about thirty taxi drivers clamoring for my attention and the honor of being able to take me to my hotel. I chose one of the nicer-looking chaps, one I outweighed by thirty pounds, and gave him my suitcase to put in the trunk. I climbed in the back seat and settled down to enjoy the ride.

The drive to the hotel took twenty minutes, and on the way, the Lord appeared to me in a vision and told me to do the smartest thing I've ever done in my life. I took from my wallet two hundred lira in small denominations, folded the bills, and put them in my shirt pocket.

We pulled up in front of my hotel, and I got out and waited for him to get my suitcase.

"How much?" I asked.

"Three hundred lira!" he said stoutly, with a perfectly straight face.

"The information guy at the airport told me the price was one hundred fifty lira," I said.

He started shouting and shaking his head, and almost jumping up and down about the price of gasoline, sick children, car repairs, and I don't know what all, and I held up my hand to stop him. With my other hand, I took out the money I had put in my shirt pocket.

With both hands, I spread the money out like a bridge hand, so he could see it easily, and said, "Here is two hundred lira." (I didn't mind being cheated a little.) "Will you take that?"

He jumped up and down, even worse than before, shouting and almost crying and I looked around nervously, hoping none of his tough friends would come out of a nearby alley and rough me up.

"Absolutely not!" he finished in a huff.

I made sure he was watching and very slowly, I took out ten lira and put it back in my shirt pocket. I spread the money out again and said, "Now, here is one hundred ninety lira. Will you take that?"

Quick as a flash, he took the remaining money from my hands and with a big smile said, "Thank you very much!" He got back in his car and drove off in a very happy mood.

He wasn't the only happy one. I wiped the sweat from my brow, picked up my bag, and went into the hotel. Dodged another bullet.

Man's Best Friend

In the olden days, when I had a telephone and even answered it on occasion, I got a call from my friend, Bill, who was coming from Illinois to have a voice lesson with our distinguished and very famous teacher, Margaret Harshaw.

"We'll just be there for the afternoon," he said, "and I have a huge favor to ask."

"No problem, what is it?"

"I'd like to leave my dog with you while we (his wife, too) work with Miss Harshaw for about two hours. It'll be early Saturday afternoon."

"That shouldn't be a problem," I lied.

I lived in a single room, not counting a very small bathroom, and keeping a dog in there with me was going to be tight. Maybe if the weather was nice, I could take him for a walk. Hell, I grew up in the country. Never in my life did I take a dog out for a walk. The dogs always lived outside, and they could take a walk whenever they wanted to. They didn't need me to go with 'em. Hell, I bet they even had a leash for the damned dog. Well, I'd agreed and I'd keep my promise.

The three of them showed up at 12:30 on Saturday afternoon, and I stepped off my front porch to greet them. They parked their car—a Volvo, for God's sake—and climbed out. Candy opened the back door, and out bounded about forty-five pounds of German Shorthaired Pointer. The dog couldn't have been over a year old, and he was overjoyed to see me. The dog reached me in three jumps and took a flying leap up and planted both front paws on my chest. I broke his momentum slightly with my left forearm and, with my right hand, tried to give him a good whack on the side of the head, but he was too fast for me. He bounced away and tore around the small front yard in an ecstatic frenzy, I guess happy to be free of the back seat of the car. Bill and Candy observed all this with proud and understanding smiles.

"He's glad to be out of the car," Bill explained.

"I don't blame him," I said. "Come on in."

They came into my room and sat down on the couch, and I sat on one of the two kitchen chairs. The dog also came inside and jumped all over everything and everybody.

"I don't suppose you'd want a beer, would you?"

They declined because of their lesson.

"I believe I'll have one, if you don't mind," and I helped myself. The prospect of spending the afternoon with the dog made me thirsty.

I don't remember the dog's name, but Bill and Candy kept telling him to quit jumping on the furniture and everybody and he ignored them completely.

"He's always like this," Bill said. "He's still just a pup and doesn't know how to behave."

"Uh-huh."

They hung around for about fifteen minutes and then said they must be off. We all went outside, and I got the idea they couldn't wait to leave me and the dog. They each gave the dog affectionate pats and told him to be a good boy while Mama and Daddy were gone. They promised to be back in just over two hours, and then they drove off.

Fido was only a tiny bit concerned when they left, and he made one quick turn around the front yard, gathering speed, and came straight for me to see if he could hit me in the chest again and, this time, knock me down. But this time, I was ready for him. He left the ground ten feet from me, and I quickly stepped toward him and raised both arms with hands clinched together and hit him as hard as I could on the left side of his chest, knocking him on the ground, flat on his back. He was very surprised but thought it was a new game and rolled to his feet for another try. He had turned his head away from me as he got up, and I had already taken a long step toward him with my left leg and, with my right foot, launched a kick that would have easily split the uprights from forty yards out. It was a mighty kick that landed right, smack-dab on his balls. Ouchadoo!

Now that I had his attention, he realized the games were over. After that, you never saw such a well-behaved dog. When Bill and Candy returned, we all went back into my room and Fido jumped on everybody and everything, except me. Inside the house, he watched me like a hawk. If I made any movement or gesture at all, he stopped whatever he was doing and gave me his full, undivided attention and was ready for instant evasive action if necessary.

"I don't understand it, Jack. That dog behaves beautifully around you and like an idiot around everybody else. How do you do that?"

"Oh, I have a way with animals, especially dogs. We got to know each other while you were gone, and we reached a mutual understanding as to how he should behave. I read him a couple of lines from the Good Book."

"I can see that. Well, I don't know what you did, but it worked."

"It usually does," I said.

The Greatest Day of My Life

On the greatest day of my life, I was called in to see the commanding officer of my company at Ft. Sill, Oklahoma. I was soon to graduate from Artillery Fire Direction School and be sent to South Vietnam as a forward observer and to die in battle by getting my ass shot off. On the average, forward observers lasted less than fifty seconds in combat situations.

"Everton!" he said. "The war is winding down and we are not going to need you in Vietnam. As a college graduate, you have been promised an officer's commission, but if you were to release the army of that promise, we would shorten your enlistment by one year and send you anywhere you want to go."

Those are the most glorious two sentences I have ever heard in all my long life. I remained calm and stoic.

"Where do I sign?"

"The papers are being drawn up for you and several others, and all of you will report back here at 1600 hours this afternoon. You can sign at that time. And by the way, where would you like to be sent?"

"To Germany," I said without my hesitation.

"Very well. That will be all."

I saluted and left.

And in that space of two or three minutes, my life changed direction and focus, and the ramifications of the fortuitous opportunity and the quick decision made continue to exert a major influence on my life and thought to this present day.

The Army made good on its end of the deal, and on my way to Germany I stopped off at Ft. Dix., New Jersey, to help the troops there pick up about six hundred pounds of cigarette butts. Actually, the six hundred pounds was only my contribution. I don't know how many butts the others picked up, but after six months of basic training and advanced artillery fire control school, I was well qualified to do the job, and I did it right. While I was there, I was called into another important commander's office for a short interview, and the sergeant behind the desk was looking at my records, or whatever.

"I see you have a degree in music."

"That's correct." (It was one of the reasons I picked up butts so well, but I didn't bring it up at that time.)

"The Seventh Army has an orchestra in Berlin. How would you like to go there?"

"That would be fine, but I'm a singer, not an instrumentalist," I explained.

"They have a chorus in Heidelberg."

"Send me to Heidelberg," I said, and that was that.

A few days later, I boarded a plane to Frankfurt am Main, where I then boarded an army bus to Heidelberg, about an hour's drive to the south. I could not believe my good luck, although I had been due some. Heidelberg was, and still is, considered one of the most beautiful and romantic cities in all of Germany.

Heading south, we had not been on the bus for more than fifteen minutes when we pulled into a highway rest stop. Our German chaperone got out of the bus and opened up the side luggage compartment and took out two cases of beer, which he brought back inside and set on the floor next to the driver. He then proceeded to pass out bottles of beer to anyone who wanted to sample the delicious taste of German hospitality. I could tell that I was going to appreciate being in the American Army much more in Germany than in the United States.

When we arrived in Heidelberg, I reported to the office of the Seventh Army Soldiers' Chorus, and they gave me an audition time for late the next morning. I slept in a guest room at Patton Barracks and showed up the next day at the appointed hour. I had not sung a note, not counting army marching songs, in six months, and I certainly had not had a chance to practice. They had a capable-looking accompanist, and he asked what I wanted to sing.

"'Pieta, rispetto, onore,' from *Macbeth*," I answered.

I watched him closely to see his reaction. He nodded and said he needed to go get the music. I was impressed that he obviously knew the great baritone aria and that they had the sheet music somewhere on the premises. I felt good about that. Made me comfortable.

The captain/conductor and three or four section leaders were present, and I sang the shit out of it, including the high A-flat at the end. It was an audition that would have put Ettore Bastianini to shame. I was singing for my life, don't you see. If I were to fail the audition, I would be crawling through the snow six months of the year, somewhere up on the East German border. "Playing Army," we called it. No thanks. Picking up cigarette butts, crawling around in the dirt and snow, getting shot at from time to time, carrying a gun and playing army does wonders for your high notes. I mean, it keeps you focused. I never sang better.

I got the job and they gave me thirty days to learn the substantial amount of music that was the standard repertoire for the concerts—everything from Gregorian Chant, Stravinsky, and Broadway to "Dogface Soldier."

For a year and a half, I sang with the chorus throughout Germany, the Netherlands, and Belgium, and we made one trip to Barcelona. We averaged at least three concerts a week, and we practiced six or seven hours a day when we were not performing. There were some outstanding musicians in the group, but most of us were just regular guys who could carry a tune. And yet, with all that practice, most of the time we sang very well. When we weren't practicing or performing, we drank a heck of a lot of beer—a good, honest, patriotic activity—and we did that very well, too. I must admit that due to the influences of the fine musicians in the group and the constant practice and performing, I came out of the army a much better singer than I was when I went in. It was a remarkable turn of good fortune when you consider what could have happened to me.

During my Heidelberg days, I met my two best friends, Jim and John, and they remain my best friends to this day, forty years later. After our military service, they went straight to Vienna to study at the Musikhochschule, and I joined them after I studied two years at Indiana University. Ah, the many things we have done together! But those are other stories I will tell on another day.

I hated the army and that I was forced to participate in such a chickenshit institution in order to "serve my country," still rankles. Nevertheless, through no fault of the army's, there were positive things that happened to me during the twenty-two months I was a soldier. It all happened, because at that time, on the greatest day of my life, I went to Europe, instead of Southeast Asia, "and that has made all the difference."